THE GREEN · TIGER'S CARAVAN

An annual gathering
of stories, poems, and entertainment
for the young

A Star & Elephant Book
The Green Tiger Press
La Jolla 1982

First Edition
First Printing
ISBN 0-914676-32-6

THE GREEN TIGER'S CARAVAN

Every year we receive in the mail thousands of manuscripts and illustrations from writers and artists who want us to publish them. Most of them we cannot use. A few we make into books. Others are deserving of publication, but are too small to make into a book. These excellent small things we have gathered into this Caravan. We have added drawings, games and puzzles from *Saint Nicholas* (1873-1939), the greatest of children's magazines, and a few from *The Book of Five Hundred Puzzles* (1859) and *Sunny Yellow Puzzle Book*.

Compiled by the editorial staff of The Green Tiger Press

CONTENTS

The Very Worst Baker in the World

by Maxine Schur
illustrated by Jeff Carnehl

Long ago in a small village lived a poor baker and his wife. Now, you may wonder how a baker could be poor. After all, everyone needs bread. But people are full of surprises. This baker was poor because hardly anyone would buy his bread. He was the very worst baker in the world. The very worst!

His cupcakes came out like doorknobs and his cookies like weights. When he couldn't remember what went into his dough, he tossed in sawdust or candlewax. Once, in a panic, he threw the alarm clock into a pumpernickel, and his own bread woke him early the next morning.

"So?" you ask. "What about his wife? She was a sensible woman, surely. Could she not have made a little money sewing or knitting for the villagers?" Well, the Baker's wife, poor soul, was the worst seamstress in the whole world! If you wanted her to make your shirt long enough so, if it isn't asking too much, you could tuck it into your trousers, she'd sew it down to your knees. If you wanted a nice handkerchief, you'd get one ... the size of a postage stamp, maybe smaller.

And her knitting! Such knitting shouldn't even be mentioned, but I will just say that the poor woman once knitted old Mr. Geezer's socks to Widow Carraway's knickers, and, since neither customer could agree where to separate the two garments, they decided to marry and share the darn thing.

Now you see why the Baker and his wife didn't have many customers. Few people like eating waxy bread or wearing socks which tickle their chins.

This year summer came early to the small village, blazing into town like a gold chariot. Never had a summer been so brilliant. The earth glowed with color and life, while the air was as still as a dream.

Men and women sweated from the heat and had to rest often from their work. Children could play outside only for a few minutes or the sun would burn them pink. Everybody felt the sun's strength, especially the Baker and his wife. Their home was above the bakery. It had a rusty old tin roof that trapped the heat like a baking sheet. With the bakehouse oven raging below and the sun burning above, the little house was unbearably hot. Though his wife complained her needle was almost too hot to hold, the Baker had it worse. Working next to his raging fire, he was miserable. At times he felt he would simply melt ... drip slowly away like a candle that no one bothers to put out.

"If only we had a nicer house," the wife said one evening at supper. "You know, dear, cool and strong and oh ... wouldn't it be lovely to have a verandah so we could sit out in rocking chairs on summer nights and look at the moon!"

"Would be charming," the Baker agreed. "But we're lucky we have any house at all. Besides, Wife, come winter and we'll be cursing the cold. Think on that!"

" 'Tis so, I suppose." The wife sighed and fanned herself sadly with a stale slice of bread.

Now it so happened it was almost time for the midsummer festival. Every year the villagers put on a festival to give thanks for the gifts of the land: the fruits, the vegetables, the flowers, the birds. The festival was going to be more beautiful than ever this year because

1

The Green Tiger's Caravan

the King, yes, that's right, the King himself, was coming to the village. Folks were gossiping themselves silly about the King's visit. You didn't need ears to hear their chatter.

"Is it true the King will choose a bride at the festival?"

"No, but I heard the King will give a skin of wine to every villager!"

"And I heard the King is going to wear a cloak of ostrich feathers and will arrive in a carriage of solid gold!"

One morning while the village was preparing itself for the royal visit, a loud knocking was heard at the Baker's door. When the Baker opened it, he found a richly dressed man standing there, shouting as he read from a parchment scroll.

"Hear Ye! Hear Ye! Hear Ye! Be it known that His Royal Highness, the King, hereby orders that the Baker, being the only baker in the village, make a special midsummer festival bread for the King's banquet table!"

"Oh," the Baker breathed.

"Silence! I haven't finished," the messenger snapped.

"Be it known that the Baker's wife, being the only seamstress in the village, will sew a special handkerchief embroidered with many colors by which the King can remember the festival."

"Good gracious, me!" his wife exclaimed.

"Those are His Majesty's orders. Mark them well!" And without so much as a "Good day to you all," the King's messenger was on his horse and galloping fast into the distant dust.

"Surely, life is full of surprises!" the Baker's wife cried as she shut the door. "Fancy the King wanting *us* to bake his bread and sew his handkerchief!"

" 'Tis a grand honor. Any fool can see that, my dear, but I fear greatly that our sort of handiwork could not please anyone ... let alone a King!"

The Baker and his wife were immediately so sobered by this truth, they slumped into two chairs and stared at each other without speaking for a long, long while. Finally the Baker stood up and said slowly, "It is my duty to bake the King's bread, and since I can't get any worse, I can only get better ... so I will! I will bake the best loaf of bread ever to be found in the land!"

Then the Baker's wife jumped up and cried, "And it is *my* duty to sew the King's handkerchief, so I will. And by my threads and needles, if I don't sew the prettiest handkerchief ever made for a King!"

"This time, Wife, I'm going to read the recipe downside up and upside down till I get it right!" the Baker boasted.

"And I'm going to measure the length and width of the King's handkerchief a hundred times or more!" his wife declared proudly.

Then the Baker bowed to his wife and she curtsied low, and the two linked arms and did a funny little dance around and around the chairs. Around and around they went, and then, around and around again.

The hot summer days melted quickly away. The whole village was busy preparing for the festival: decorating buildings, cooking food, brewing festival punch, cleaning the streets, rounding up the stray dogs, and stitching festival clothes. Everyone was working hard to make things extra nice, for it isn't every day a King comes to visit.

The day before the festival, while his wife was putting the finishing touches on the royal handkerchief, the Baker was in the bakehouse preparing the dough for the King's bread. All day he had been feverishly sifting and measuring and sifting again. He grew hot and tired, but just as he was reading the recipe for the 39th time, there came a loud banging at the bakehouse door.

The Very Worst Baker in the World

"Not another royal messenger!" hoped the Baker. But when he opened it, millions of dust particles and Barnaby, the chimney sweep, drifted in. Barnaby was the Baker's good friend. He was as tall and scraggly as his chimney broom and much dirtier.

"Hello Barnaby, what brings you here?"

"My feet do," answered Barnaby, who enjoyed a joke.

"Um ... um ..." the Baker mumbled, "um ... well, um ... How are you then? ... um ... three cups of flour ..."

"My business is reduced to ashes and I've got a bad case of the flue, but the rich Lady Docket gave me a big jug of midsummer wine. You might care to share a sip with me?"

"Um ... er ... five cups of yeast ... er ... sorry Barnaby, old friend," the Baker answered, "but I'm too busy. The King has commanded me to bake him a very special bread, and it must be perfect ... Now was that eighteen cups of flour or eighty?"

"I suppose you knead the dough!" Barnaby said and he threw back his head and laughed loudly, showing two lines of broken teeth that reminded the Baker of rows of dirty chimneys.

"Look here, Barnaby, I haven't got time for jokes. Can't you see I've got work to do here? Nothing must go wrong. Nothing! ... er ... uh ... let me see ... forty spoons of sugar ... and one hundred cups of yeast ... bake for thirty minutes or three?"

"Now where's the harm in a little cooling wine for chimney's sake! Fresh and tasty. A tiny drop will refresh you ... make your work a lot easier. Eh?"

"Well ... well ... all right, Barnaby," the Baker sighed, "But only a wee drop."

Barnaby handed the wine to the Baker. The Baker took a sip. "Not bad!" he smiled, and then he took another. "Yes, not bad at all! ... so ... um ... 64½ spoons of salt and, I think, two hundred cups of yeast ... Barnaby, I'll have just a drip more."

The Baker took a drink and then another. "Ahhh, there's nothing finer than midsummer wine!" he proclaimed. He took another sip and then another and another and then another. "Oh, truly delicious!" he declared. "Now, that's two hundred cups of yeast ... or was that buckets ...?"

While Barnaby and the Baker were busy telling jokes and drinking more and more drops of wine, up above the bakehouse, the Baker's wife had already sewn sixty-three lace flowers around the edge of the King's handkerchief. She was beginning to feel sleepy. "I'll sew just a little more until my husband comes up," she told herself. But the fiery hot day slowly burned itself into cinder black night and still the Baker did not return home.

"How long can he take?" his wife grumbled. "I'll sew just a wee bit more until he comes in."

So the Baker's wife sewed and sewed and then she sewed and sighed and sighed and sighed and sewed, then snored and sighed and sewed and snored ... and so on, far into the night.

When morning came, the sun glared like an angry man at the window. It shone into the tired eyes of the wife and rudely woke her up. Then she realized her husband had not come home.

"Why, oh, why hasn't he come in? Oh, Heaven save him from his own foolishness!"

But there was nothing she could do. Another royal messenger stood knocking at the door.

"Hear Ye! Hear Ye! Hear Ye!" the messenger barked. "His Majesty requests his gifts to be presented on his arrival at the festival: first the royal handkerchief, then the royal bread. Make haste, woman!" the messenger advised. "A King waits for no one!"

The Baker's wife wrapped the handkerchief carefully between sheets of baking paper and hurried off to the festival. As she ran, she prayed that her husband was already there.

The Green Tiger's Caravan

The festival was in full swing when she arrived. Clowns were punching their own noses and running on their hands. Twelve jugglers were juggling hats and fishcakes. A large black bear was dancing the tarantella, and the minstrels, well, they were singing love songs to everyone.

In the early morning sunshine all the villagers were at the fairgrounds, laughing and dancing and kicking up dust. Then suddenly from far away there came a faint sound of trumpets, and someone cried, "The King! the King! Make way for the King!"

And sure enough, the King was riding into town. Fifty royal horsemen prancing in front and fifty royal horsemen in back. My, the whispers! The nudges! The finger pointing! The giggles! The open mouths! Anyone would have thought the King wasn't at all a person who blows his nose like you and I.

When the royal coach reached the fairgrounds, the King stepped out and stood upon a silver platform where everyone could see him. He read a short speech and then he called for his gifts.

"Fetch me the Royal Festival Handkerchief!" he bellowed.

The Baker's wife stumbled forward. "Your Majesty, Highness, Sir," she began nervously, "I have the great honor to present you with ..." But before she could finish, a giant shadow was cast across the fairgrounds. "Help! It's coming! Help! It's coming!!!"

At once everyone fell to shrieking and shouting. Some people fainted and those who didn't scattered like chickens, screaming as they ran. While the King and the Baker's wife were trying to figure it out, they caught a glimpse of "it."

It was a yellowish blob made of some horrible gloopy stuff and was about the size of a small house. It whistled and wobbled through the hot streets, lurching toward the fairgrounds, sticking and smacking and stretching as it went. It had bad breath, sweaty damp skin, and every second it was growing bigger. When it had grown to the size of a large house, it began to make noises and shove people about.

"Burple. Hurble. Bubble. Sneep!" It belched in Lady Docket's face.

"Glipple. Stickle. Bleeple. Slurp!" It spat at Butcher Fife.

The King, meantime, took to his heels, as did the Baker's wife. In fact, the whole village was going crazy trying to get away from the monstrous blob. Those who could climbed trees, while others hid behind locked doors.

"Help! Help! We'll be flattened like pancakes! We'll be crushed like crumbs!" screamed the Olberti brothers as the blob cornered them in an alley. But too late! The last the horrified villagers saw of the two brothers, they were gobbled up by the blob like sausages.

Now the people were really wild, for they were not only frightened but angry. Little Sally Smithsdale ran from her hiding place and lashed at the blob with her jump rope.

"Bad, bad blob!" she cried.

"Sally, dear, don't do that!" her mother screamed. But too late! The ill-mannered blob burped in little Sally's face, then swallowed her whole, jump rope and all, pulling her in like a fish on a line.

"Kill it! Kill it!" people shouted, standing on roofs. But it was no use. The blob was almost as large and noisy as the tavern. It slobbered over gardens and hedges. It flattened Tanner Dobble's pansy beds. It wrapped itself drunkenly around eight lamp posts and forced its way into the public lavatory. Everywhere the blob waddled, it left a mess behind. The townspeople feared their village would be destroyed, but they did not know what to do.

Just then the Baker arrived at the fairgrounds, unshaven and sleepy eyed. When he saw the monster blob try to push its way into the town hall, he cried, "Great shortening! 'Tis my bread!" He knew there was only one way to stop it. If he had an oven to bake it solid, it could then be contained and later, perhaps, sliced. But he couldn't think of any oven in the village

4

The Very Worst Baker in the World

that was big enough. He was still thinking when his wife spotted him.

"Where have you been?" she cried. "Are you all right, dear? Why didn't you come home last night? Were you captured by the blob? Oh! I'm so happy you're alive!"

"Thank you, my dear. I ... er ... I fell asleep in the bakehouse. You see, Barnaby and I had a wee tiny drop of midsummer wine and ... uh ... well ... as for the blob, *that* is the King's bread."

The Baker's wife stared at the blob, and then she stared at her husband. And then she burst into tears.

"You Tom Fool Noodle!" she cried. "The King will behead us! He'll lock us in the dungeon forever! He'll punish us for certain!"

She cried and she cried, and all the while she cried, the midsummer sun blazed and raged in the sky. The sun burned so strongly, it almost seemed the sky itself would catch fire.

Then, a most amazing thing happened. The Baker's blob began to move more and more slowly and more and more quietly. When it reached the gates of the city, it let out one last gasp. It stopped waddling. It stopped pushing. It didn't even breathe! Its skin slowly lost its dampness and began to harden. Slowly, oh, so slowly, it turned the rich bright color of a copper penny.

The blob was gone.

In its place, standing warm and sweet smelling, was a beautiful loaf of bread — or rather, a beautiful GIANT loaf of bread. The hot sun had baked it solid, through and through. Its hard crust twinkled in the sunlight, and a wonderful smell of fresh bread floated all over the village.

People cautiously came out of their hiding places. The first to approach the bread was the Baker. Working with a large bread knife, he carved out a deep tunnel. The Olberti brothers and little Sally Smithsdale crawled out. They were greeted by the welcoming cheers of the crowd. Happily, they were none the worse for their mishap, looking only a little pastyfaced from an unhappy attempt to eat their way out.

Once again the royal bugles were blown. The King, who had been hiding all the while under the royal coach, now came riding on horseback. The brave King rode right up to the tame and sweet smelling bread.

"What's this?" he asked. The Baker stepped forward nervously. "That, your Majesty ... that is ... er ... your bread ... uh ... unfortunately."

"Thunderous Thrones!" the King cried. "It's as big as a house! "My bread is as big as a house!" Then the King began to laugh. He threw back his head and laughed and laughed. Lady Docket and the Olberti brothers laughed too. Soon everyone was laughing ... even the Baker. They all laughed so hard that tears rolled down their faces, and pretty soon they all had to blow their noses.

"Ha! Ha! A bread as big as a house!" the King roared. "Wonderful surprise! Wonderful! Baker, forget my order. You may keep this bread. Perhaps if you hollow it out, you could live in it. Ha! Ha! Merry Midsummer to both of you!"

"Thank you, Your Majesty," the Baker answered shyly. He was thrilled to receive such a big present, even if it was his own bread.

"But now, what about the Royal Festival Handkerchief?" The King turned to the Baker's wife with a penetrating eye.

"Gracious! I have it right here, Your Royal Person." She began to unfold the handkerchief, which she had been clutching all the while. "I worked on it all night, Sir King, I ..."

But she got no further. The crowd began laughing all over again. The King was uncontrollable. The Baker's wife had unrolled a colorful handkerchief as wide and as long as a blanket!

The Very Worst Baker in the World

"My thimbles!" she blushed. "I must have counted wrongly!"

"Never mind," the King chuckled. "It will, no doubt, make lovely curtains for your new home. Merry Midsummer!"

"Oh, thank you, Your Big Highness!" she said. She thought he was really a very nice King.

When the festival had ended, the Baker and his wife, with the help of their friend, Barnaby, carved out the inside of the giant bread. Then they cut out doors, a few windows, a chimney, and even a verandah. It was cool and spacious and the new lace curtains looked charming.

"We're lucky people, aren't we, dear?" the wife said to the Baker as they swept the last crumbs out the door. "That we are!" the Baker replied. "That we are!"

But he had spoken too soon. A few nights after the festival, they heard shouts and chants outside their windows. They heard tapping and rapping at their door. When the Baker opened the door, he was amazed to see hundreds of people, perhaps the whole village, holding signs and singing. The songs were short and sharp, and the villagers sang them over and over again.

One group sang,

    "For our sake,   "If we ache with your cake,

    Do not bake!"   and We'll be dead with your bread!"

While another group sang,

    "You're not our foe,   "Woe to us,

    But please don't sew!" and If you sew for us!"

The message was all too clear. The villagers were so frightened by this last adventure, they were now asking the Baker and his wife to stop baking and sewing altogether.

"But," the Baker said meekly to the mayor, "my good wife and I must live somehow!"

"We're not meaning to starve you, man," the mayor explained gently. "It's just that we'd prefer you both do something else in our village other than baking or sewing. 'Tis too dangerous! Now, good night to you."

As the Baker closed the door, he heard a woman in the crowd yell back, "Think of the children!"

That night, they tossed unhappily in their sleep. How could they live without their work? Then the Baker's wife woke with an idea. She crept out of bed and scurried quietly down to the bakehouse. She rolled up her sleeves and got to work.

The next morning, the Baker awoke to a delicious smell. He went down to the bakehouse and saw his wife standing at the counter, serving a long line of customers that curled around the corner. When he saw, not only the little brown loaves of bread nestled on the counter, as warm and brown as puppies, but the fine cakes and pies, he knew that, from that day on, his wife would do all the baking.

As for the Baker, there was nothing for him but to take up sewing. He worked at it like a schoolboy and soon he learned to love the firm thrust and pull of a nimble needle. Before long, he had become the best tailor in the kingdom. He did embroidery, knitting, and needle-point. He must have had a hidden talent.

Someone once told me that when the King married, it was the Baker who sewed the wedding clothes and the Baker's wife who baked the Royal Wedding Cake.

So, there you are.

The very worst baker in the world was married to the very worst seamstress, and the very best pastry chef in the world was married to the very best tailor.

And they were the same two people.

Ah, people are so full of surprises!

The Throw

by M. Lawrence Miller

Two birds with one small stone I killed,
I was a clever fellow!
Four hopping frogs, six green balloons,
Eight bumblebees, bright yellow;

Ten purple kites, twelve weather vanes,
That stone that I let loose it's
Slicing off the doorknobs from
Vermont to Massachusetts.

Chasing foxes through the fields,
Zooming under noses,
Flying down the garden lanes,
Mowing down red roses.

Across the land I hurled that stone
Toward the shining sea,
David with his slingshot
Was not half the lad as me!

Across the mighty ocean,
Poking holes in gallant sails,
Denting secret periscopes,
And mystifying whales.

Six inches off the English soil
Along it hurtled madly,
Puncturing the pumpkin crop
Just south of London badly.

Instantly I'd won such fame,
My face on magazines,
That invitations showered in
From Governors and Queens.

O, I was such a huge success
That every Judge and dunce
Signed a great petition
To crown me King at once!

"The arm that made the strongest throw
That history has recorded,
Should steer our noble Ship of State
And all of those aboard it!"

The way ahead was smooth and clear,
No obstacles were showing,
No finer fellow ever lived,
The future looked so glowing.

Unfortunately the world is round,
A simple fact, you see.
That stone that killed the two small birds,
That stone that I set free,
Came whizzing round the wondrous earth
And did the same to me.

1. A riddle, a riddle—now who am I?
   Long tail, no head and a single eye?

2. Why may a sailor be expected to know what goes on in the moon?

3. What is it that the more you take from it,
   the larger it grows?

4. Why may carpenters believe there is no such
   thing as stone?

5. How do we know the public library is the tallest building
   in your town?

6. Where is the largest diamond in the
   town?

7. What runs without feet and never
   leaves its bed?

8. What is it by losing an eye has only
   a nose left?

9. Why is it unsafe to keep a clock on the
   stairs?

10. 'Tis very precious and, strange though true,
    You can give it away and keep it, too.
    If it is good, 'tis well to make it.
    If you are good, you will never break it.

11. Not all inks are made to write with,
    As you may have thought was true.
    Just guess the names of these and see
    What some of them can do.
    1. An ink that is made with the eye.
    2. An ink that is made with the mind.
    3. An ink that you skate in.
    4. An ink that is the very edge.
    5. An ink for thirsty people.
    6. An ink that is an animal.

12. When is a farmer cruel to his corn?

Answers, p. 88

9

That's My Herbie

by Nathan Zimelman
illustrated by Susan Tereba

"Herbie Harrison III," said Mrs. Herbert Harrison II, mother, "you eat like a bird."

Herbie sliced a large potato in two. The bigger piece he speared with his fork.

"When people say that," Herbie chewed noisily, "they mean that you're not eating so good. I'm eating good." He speared several large and buttery peas to go with the smaller piece of potato and raised his fork.

"What some people do not know, your mother knows," said Mrs. Harrison. "I know that birds eat exceedingly well. In addition, Herbie," Mrs. Harrison pointed at Harold, the canary, who was flying about his cage madly, "they exercise. There are no fat birds. You, Herbie, will be the first fat bird, ever."

"Mother." For a moment Herbie had stopped eating. He had to, because he was using his fork to point at the family cat, William the Conqueror, who was crouching like a lion, his eyes upon Herbie. "Why is he doing that?"

"Perhaps he thinks that you are a bird." Mrs. Harrison began a laugh which she did not complete. "Herbie," she shrieked, "you *are* a bird!"

William the Conqueror's back arched, his fur rose into exclamation marks, and he rushed yowling from the room.

"If I am a bird," asked Herbie, "why is William the Conqueror running from me?"

"Because," said Mrs. Harrison, "you are a very large bird."

Harold, the canary, sang a challenge to the cat to come back and fight him and his large friend.

Herbie hopped to a mirror to see for himself.

"I am a bird," he cried, "with feathers as blue as my clothes were blue."

"Would your dear mother lie to you?" Carefully Mrs. Harrison selected a hat. "Come, Herbie," she held out her hand, "for this you need more than a mother's love. We will go ask Dr. O'Briedly why. Herbie, stop pecking at the crumbs on the table. You have eaten enough."

Into a morning street full of prowling cats and trembling birds went Herbie and his mother.

"Isn't it nice, Herbie," smiled Mrs. Harrison, "how the birds come down from the trees and walk with you."

"The cats," said Herbie, "are going the other way, up the trees, and crouching, shaking."

Together, Herbie and the birds told the cats a thing or two.

"That is not nice, Herbie," said Mrs. Harrison putting a finger to her lips. "You know many fine cats. Just because you have become a bird doesn't mean that you should forget your manners. Sir! Sir!" Waving, Mrs. Harrison began to run. "Do please wait, Mr. Bus Driver! Hurry, Herbie. Hurry."

Herbie flapped. Birds rose about him. "You go ahead, mother. I'll fly over and meet you there."

"You are too young to fly by yourself," Mrs. Harrison fluttered her arms, "and I am too old to start." Mrs. Harrison skipped and jumped and for a moment was airborne. "Almost. Anyway, the bus has stopped. Hop up the stairs, Herbie."

The Green Tiger's Caravan

The bus driver stuck out his arm so the way into the bus was blocked. "What you got there, lady?"

"My son, Herbie Harrison III, a perfectly normal young American boy."

Mrs. Herbert Harrison II, mother, brushed the bus driver's arm aside and firmly marched herself and Herbie to a seat.

The bus driver shrugged. "So why not a big bluebird?"

With a crunch the bus started, and surrounded by birds off it rode.

"Do you wish to sit by the window, Herbie?" Mrs. Harrison asked.

"Everybody's looking," said Herbie.

"Naturally," said Mrs. Harrison. "There are not many bluebirds to be seen in a city. Ring the bell, Herbie. We have arrived at our destination."

"How?" asked Herbie.

"You have a perfectly good beak, Herbie," said his mother.

Off the bus hopped Herbie and Mrs. Harrison, and, surrounded by birds, they hurried off and up and into Dr. O'Briedly's office.

"And what do we find wrong with us today?" Dr. O'Briedly peered through his spectacles.

"Well, Dr. O'Briedly," said Mrs. Harrison, "you probably won't believe this but ..."

Dr. O'Briedly held up a hand. "Stop, dear lady, I can see. Your son Herbie fell into a snow-drift and has turned a frozen blue."

The sun beat upon the window. The air conditioner whirred and whirred.

"It is July, doctor," said Mrs. Harrison.

"Then why is it so cold that my spectacles have frosted over?"

Briskly Dr. O'Briedly polished his spectacles. He perched them on his nose and peered through the thickness of the glass. He blinked once and twice. He looked again. "Mrs. Harrison, I am a people doctor," said Dr. O'Briedly. "Why have you brought a large bluebird to my office?"

"He has changed," Mrs. Harrison took a comb from her purse and combed the feathers on Herbie's head. "But he is still my Herbie."

"For this Herbie you need a bird doctor." Dr. O'Briedly shivered. "Which is just as well, Mrs. Harrison. I always leave for Florida when the weather turns cold."

Mrs. Harrison left Dr. O'Briedly's office and took the elevator to the ground floor. Since there was no room for even one more, Herbie flew.

"Was that enjoyable, Herbie?" Mrs. Harrison asked.

"Mother," Herbie flapped his wings, "it was like your blueberry waffles."

"That delightful?" smiled Mrs. Harrison. "Still, we will find a bird doctor and have my Herbie made into a boy again. What am I talking about? We have a bird doctor."

"Are we going to Harold the canary's doctor?" asked Herbie loudly, so he could be heard above the birds that were twittering all about them.

"You can never go to where you have already arrived." Mrs. Harrison opened a door. "And here we are."

There was a selection of animals and people waiting on seats and on the floor. But no sooner had Mrs. Harrison and Herbie entered than the animals who were on the floor jumped up onto the seats and huddled small in their owners' arms.

"Is something wrong?" inquired Mrs. Harrison.

"Wrong? Wrong? I should say there is something wrong." A small person in a white coat jumped up and down beneath Herbie's beak. "He's wrong. That's what's wrong. Your large bluebird is frightening all of my tiny patients."

"There is one that doesn't mind." Mrs. Harrison waved at a canary that was glowering

That's My Herbie

through the bars of its cage at a Siamese cat.

"Oh, what does he know." The animal doctor stamped his foot. "All songbirds are brainless."

If a bluebird can growl, Herbie growled. The doctor jumped into a plump lady's arms.

"Go, go," he waved. "If there's something wrong with him, take him to a zoo. They don't mind large creatures."

"My son, Herbie," frowned Mrs. Harrison, "is not a creature. However, it is a pleasant day. The sun shines its warm welcome. We shall stroll to the zoo."

In a whirl of colors and surrounded by song, Herbie and his mother strolled to the zoo.

"I see the lions," said Mrs. Harrison when they arrived. "I see the tigers. I do see elephants and others. But where are the birds?"

"The sign," Herbie waved a wing, "says that the aviary is over there."

"A word of four syllables and Herbie knows what it means." Proudly Mrs. Herbert Harrison II, mother, spoke to the world. "And the animal doctor said that songbirds are brainless. Does a hawk know what A-V-I-A-R-Y means? Can a hawk even read AVIARY?"

"A hawk, my good woman, cannot read any word." A pipe followed by a man appeared from between bushes.

"Who, sir, are you?" asked Mrs. Harrison.

"I am the keeper of all this." The pipe drew a circle within which there cawed and crowed and screeched and sang a universe of birds.

"How do you do," said Mrs. Harrison. "Herbie, mind your manners."

"You don't have to push," said Herbie. "Hello, mister."

"He talks." The pipe man bit the stem of his pipe in two.

"Since he was six months old," said Mrs. Herbert Harrison II, mother.

"How did you train a bluebird to talk?" excitedly asked the pipe man.

"Whatever do you mean?" said Mrs. Harrison. "This is my son, Herbie Harrison III."

The pipe man scratched his nose with the half of his pipe. "A bluebird is your son?"

"Ever since this morning when I said 'Herbie, you eat like a bird.' Thank goodness I didn't say 'Herbie, you eat like a pig.' "

The pipe man walked around and around Herbie. "Remarkable. Remarkable."

"It's the Brightly in him," said Mrs. Harrison. "I am the former Miss Esmeralda Brightly."

"Remarkable." The pipe man took a tape measure from out of a pocket and measured Herbie from blue feathered tip down to yellow bird's feet.

"If he could be a little less remarkable and a little more Herbie," said Mrs. Harrison, "it would be so much nicer."

"My good woman, a bird is a bird and will ever be a bird."

The pipe man held a thing of blue in the gold of the sun. It was a bird's feather. Herbie's feather. Happily the song birds flew about singing. The birds of prey moved into the dark of their cages, away from the largeness of Herbie. Tears formed in each of Mrs. Harrison's eyes.

"Forever?" plaintively asked Mrs. Harrison.

Herbie pecked away his mother's tears. "Don't worry," said Herbie. "I'll always be your Herbie. But they need me too."

Herbie trilled a note to the song birds who sang even more gaily. "All their lives they've got to be afraid of cats, and hunting birds, and just about everyone. Now they've got me, big Herbie, the biggest bluebird that ever was. I'll protect them, and there will be singing and joy like there never was before."

Herbie hopped, and then hopped again. He spread his wings and fluttered, and in the midst of song, he soared into the sky, and the sky was a sudden happiness.

"That's my Herbie," proudly beamed Mrs. Herbert Harrison II, mother.

13

Snowflake Snowflake

by Peter Neumeyer

"Impossible, impossible, impossible," said Andrew's father. "Never, never, anywhere in the world can you find two snowflakes that are exactly alike."

"Not somewhere?" asked Andrew.

"Not anywhere," said his father.

"I've seen them exactly the same size," said Andrew.

"Size is not everything," said his father.

"I've seen them the same shape," said Andrew.

"Shape is not everything," said his father. "And if they were the same shape, then they were probably not the same size."

"What if they were the same shape and the same size?" asked Andrew.

"If two snowflakes were the same shape and the same size — and that would be strange indeed — one would be more wet than the other. Or one would be more dry than the other."

"Nowhere? Ever? Are you sure?" asked Andrew.

"Nowhere, ever, I am sure." said his father.

Andrew got ready. He took his magnifying glass. He took his small jam glass. He took his toothpick. He put on his galoshes, his warmest coat, his mittens and he went out in the storm.

The blizzard blew. Black tree ribs cracked with the ice. The sun was in another place. And it was cold, cold.

Even in mittens, Andrew's hands were frozen and numb. His hands were clumsy. He could not really bend his fingers. But ever so carefully with his toothpick Andrew picked up one snowflake, then another.

He looked at them carefully — there in the cold — through his magnifying glass.

The second snowflake was right. It was beautiful, small, and its points had their own points. Its outline was sharp, and Andrew could tell just exactly what it looked like. There was no question. No question at all. Though there was no sun, the snowflake glowed green, gold, blue, orange. It was so clear. It was beautiful.

Gently, with the toothpick, Andrew put his snowflake in the small jam glass.

Andrew knew his snowflake perfectly. He took it to his house. He set it carefully, in the small jam glass, just inside the front door of his house.

Again Andrew went out in the blizzard, in the snow. Cold as he was, Andrew went looking, catching the blowing, swirling, falling snowflakes on his mitten. He could hardly see, it snowed so hard.

Andrew's nose felt frozen to him, and his eyelashes were heavy white with snow, but Andrew worked on. He looked at the snowflakes on his mitten through his magnifying glass. Some were stuck together. Some had broken points, and some seemed to have none.

A few were ALMOST right — but they did not glow green, gold, blue, and orange. At least, not all those colors at once.

Andrew was so cold he could stay no longer. One last swirl he caught on his mitten.

"This will be my last chance," said Andrew, brushing off some of the snow and looking carefully as he could through his magnifying glass at nine snowflakes on his mitten.

For a second — just a second — a sunbeam glowed like icy fire. And there Andrew saw it, there on his mitten, a snowflake beautiful, small, points on its points, and glowing green, gold, blue, and orange.

Covering it, shielding the snowflake with his other mitten, Andrew rushed back, rushed home, out of the blizzard, back into his warm house, calling happily "Father, father ...."

Theodore's Uncommon Appetite

Written & Illustrated by
Jana Winthers Newman

There once was a little frog who had a very large appetite. He loved to eat little crawling things like spiders and whirligigs, and the taste of light white moths filled him with glee. But what he really found most delicious were words. He had a hunger deep down inside him for them. He couldn't help himself. It was as if he were born with the taste of words in his small pink mouth.

When he was young and not much more than a tadpole, he ate silky, tender words like WISP and OH and MY and DEARIE. As he grew, his appetite became more bold. Once, just before he became full grown, he swallowed the words WILD RED RASPBERRY. He felt his heart blink and turn in a wonderful way. It was as if certain words became a part of him.

This little frog, whose name was Theodore, loved variety. When the moon was a lemon yellow and the damselflies floated high in the starry night, Theodore swallowed pleasing combinations like HIP HIP HURRAY OWLETS IN THE AUTUMN HAY and RUN HIDE WATCH FREEZE MOCKING BIRD IN THE WILLOW TREES. And though it was not in Theodore's nature to be wasteful, on a recent holiday he was nearly unable to finish a lusty lunch of COOL STREAMS SWEET DREAMS and three rather large bumblebees.

Now you may think that Theodore grew quite happy and large, especially in light of the fact that he enjoyed plump words like LOBLOLLY with his tea and ladybugs every day at half-past four. This was not the case.

One day Theodore grew smaller with every word he swallowed. He first noticed this after devouring an entire conversation between two disagreeable toads. He suddenly felt so slight. Finally his reputation as a proud leaper lost its luster when, on a summer evening while finishing the last of the words INDIGO BUNTING BLUEBERRY HUNTING MAMA PUTS STARS ON MY WINDOWSILL, he leapt for land and came up short in the middle of the millpond.

It was not in Theodore's nature to make light of serious matters. He worried that he might get so small he would disappear altogether. But he couldn't help himself and he swallowed THE ENTIRE INDIAN OCEAN in one nervous gulp as he grew smaller still. 'What a terrible way to leave the earth,' he thought. 'Much better to be a zesty meal for some hungry heron or die as a great old sage of a frog. Simply to shrivel to a wrinkled speck is not a suitable end to life.'

One night when the moon was full, as Theodore was dozing inside a lily, he had a remarkable dream. He dreamed he was a traveler of the world. He wore a wreath of laurel leaves on his head and everywhere he went the world cried "Wonderful frog! Bravo!"

'How interesting,' he thought, still dreaming. 'Perhaps there is something about myself that I have yet to discover.'

He suddenly awoke. The rushes were stirring and the sun was a brass penny. He had fallen out of the lily and was sitting on a floating leaf. He was so startled he opened his mouth to grab a bite to eat. Instead he spoke the most beautiful poetry he had ever heard. 'How astounding,' he thought. 'Is that ME?'

16

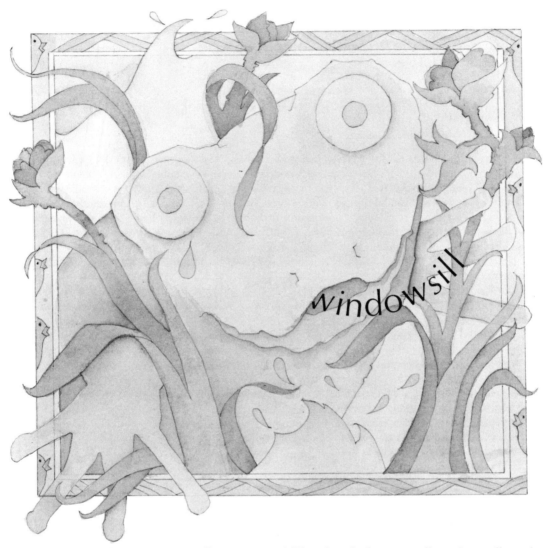

windowsill

And it was. Quite unexpectedly every word Theodore had ever swallowed now flowed like a merry celebration from his heart where he had kept it. And as each word rolled off his tongue, he approached more nearly a reasonable size for a lyrical frog. And it occurred to him how right as rain it was that he should be a poet.

And you may hear him celebrate still, if you come upon the millpond in the foggy dew of morning, when the sky is a pale color, between the nightshade and daybreak, when the light white moths are beginning to gather,

The Golden Thread

by Eugene R. Dumas
illustrated by Theresa Borelli

The hours that contain a day are static in themselves; yet they are defined by change, as wind, blowing away the still morning and spreading ripples on a calm lake, creates moments that are more than moments, a wealth of memories and emotions. Of course, not all of these moments fill the hand of happiness, and some even cause it to drain. One such moment occurs when a young boy places a possession too close to himself, closer than contentment allows, causing ripples to become waves, and day and night, no longer linear, to jam moments like ice that collects in a funnel, a narrow culvert mouth of time.

"Hi, Jeremy. What are you doing?" Conrad asked as he walked into the dimmer light of the garage.

"Look at this neat horseshoe that I found. My dad said that if I scrape off all the rust I can paint it gold with this paint that he bought for me." Jeremy held up the paint that would release his vision.

"Where did you get the horseshoe?" Conrad asked, while eyeing the treasure with a bit of envy.

"Under the porch. Do you see these holes in the horseshoe? They were plugged up with mud and rust, but now they are nearly all clear." Jeremy carried on to explain how the mud and flakes of rusting metal flew off when he first started scraping the horseshoe, and he pointed to the bare metal that was beginning to show.

Conrad envied Jeremy more and more as he watched him clean the horseshoe.

"Do you think that there will be any more of them buried under your porch?" Conrad asked, wanting one for himself.

"No, I dug all around and couldn't find any more. I guess that someone must have dropped it there by itself."

"Oh," was all Conrad could say. He wanted an equal portion of this dream and reality of a golden horseshoe.

Jeremy loosened the vise and turned the horseshoe around so that the two ends were pointing upward. As he scraped, rusty flakes flew into the air around him. After a while he stopped to poke the rust from a couple of holes.

"Can I have a try?" asked Conrad, wanting to see how hard it was to scrape.

Jeremy hesitated but was tired, so he gave the wire brush to him. Conrad scraped very hard, breaking through to the bare metal in places that were left to clean. Only when he finished the rest of the horseshoe did he hand the brush back to Jeremy. Now the horseshoe seemed partly his. He had discovered a few more nail holes and knew all the rough parts that the rust had eaten away. He wanted to keep the horseshoe for himself.

As he was thinking about such things, Conrad felt it happen: a feeling ever so slight, an almost unnoticeable trace of numbness filtered through him. It was so slight that he didn't realize what it was, and he forgot it immediately. Only in the bright sunshine could it be seen that his shadow became slightly detached from his left leg. Conrad did not even notice his disjointed shadow. It could be seen only by close observation.

Jeremy set up the horseshoe so that only one of its ends touched the vise. He then found

18

The Green Tiger's Caravan

the tiny tin of gold paint and attempted to open it, but was unsuccessful. After Conrad tried it, they decided that he would hold the can with some pliers while Jeremy pried the top off with a screw driver. On the third attempt they got it open and didn't spill any paint except from the lid as it landed face down on the work bench.

With a very small brush, Jeremy began painting the horseshoe at the end which wasn't in the vise. He slowly worked his way around the horseshoe making sure to paint underneath it, painting very carefully around the nail holes to keep paint from plugging them. Except for the two spots that touched the vise, he was finished painting in fifteen minutes.

"Well, that's all done. I guess I'll have to wait for it to dry."

In the silence they both admired the horseshoe.

"Let's go and play catch for a while," Conrad suggested.

"OK," Jeremy agreed. "You know, I think I'll get up early tomorrow morning and paint the horseshoe again before I go to school." He wished that the horseshoe would dry right away so that he wouldn't have to wait to give it another coat.

"Let's go," Jeremy said, turning to walk out the door. "You go home and get your glove and ball, and I'll get my glove."

"OK, I'll be right back." They parted at the door to meet again in a few minutes at their playing area beside the garage.

Playing catch was soothing and rhythmic, not too far removed from watching ocean waves thunder onto a beach and then slowly slide back, only to thunder again. It was not at all too soothing for Conrad, though, playing catch out there in the bright sun. He did not know that his shadow was slightly detached from his left leg, and he did not see it, but he sensed that something was wrong. While he was thinking about how he felt, he decided that he would return that night and take the horseshoe out of the garage.

Suddenly and without a sound his shadow became detached from his other leg as well. He stumbled and barely caught the ball but did not notice his shadow fell a few inches from his feet. He recovered and threw the ball back sluggishly. There was something drained out of him, something missing, a spark, an awareness, a lightness was gone.

They played for twenty minutes more, throwing high ones, fast ones, and grounders. Conrad missed too many and threw the ball wildly.

"I'm getting tired. I think I'll go home now, Jeremy," he said after recovering a ball he failed to catch.

"So am I. I'll see you at school tomorrow." Jeremy threw the ball into the air a few times as he walked toward the garage. His horseshoe was not quite dry, but by next morning he would be able to give it another coat of paint.

Conrad went home and lay down on his bed while waiting for supper. He was drowsy and restless. It was like having a dream while he was awake as he thought of stealing his best friend's horseshoe. After supper he carelessly read some comics until just before dark. Then he slipped out of the house, walked down to Jeremy's garage, stepped noiselessly inside, tucked the nearly dry horseshoe into his shirt, and went straight home. He did not have a shadow in the darkness so he did not miss it, and when he entered the house he was too preoccupied with the cool steel horseshoe touching his skin to notice that his shadow was totally gone. He quickly hid the horseshoe under his pillow, then washed, brushed his teeth, and hurried back to the darkness of his room. In the darkness a shadowless comfort was to be found.

The night passed all too quickly for Conrad. The next morning he walked the two miles to school. The sun, which Conrad felt shining through him, was searching his secrets; but all the while no shadow was to be found.

The Golden Thread

His mind was foggy, listless; his vision was clouded. He emanated this fogginess so much that neither he nor anyone near him saw that he was without a shadow, even though the sun shone and the classroom was well lit.

He avoided Jeremy all day, thankful that they were in different classes. He moped around out of tune with the activities around him. He avoided the kids in his class, who only increased the emptiness that was within him. Eyes, eyes, he knew the guilt was in his eyes. He stayed apart from the rest of his classmates until it was time to go home. Even then he didn't go straight home but went, instead, to the river that was about a half mile from his place. It was only at supper time, when he was sure that Jeremy would not be around, that Conrad returned home.

After eating he again sought refuge in his bedroom but found none, for, even in the darkness, he could not hide from himself. After going to bed he tossed and turned for a long while, knowing what he had to do.

Around midnight he finally got up, dressed, and took the horseshoe from under his pillow. He quietly left the house, and in the dim light of the street he walked to Jeremy's yard and entered into the darkness of the garage. It was in this darkness that he sought his shadow, for he had faced this darkness in the bright sunlight and was overwhelmed by it. But here, without light, he could overcome it or, at least, understand it.

He replaced the horseshoe in the vise and hurriedly walked home, still not knowing his shadow had ever left him but feeling it slowly return.

In the morning his shadow was once more full and attached. He went straight to Jeremy's house after breakfast to see if he was ready for school. Once again he found him in the garage. He was giving the horseshoe a second coat of paint.

"Hi, Jeremy."

"Hi, Conrad. Where were you yesterday?"

"I had a lot of things to do yesterday," he replied quickly.

"You know what? I forgot all about my horseshoe yesterday, so I'm painting it today instead. It sure was funny that I forgot about it like that," said Jeremy, not knowing that the shadows of friends are shared.

"The horseshoe sure is neat now, though," said Conrad, greatly relieved. The moments were once again in place; friends were friends, and the horseshoe, as bright a gold as it was, remained apart from such a friendship.

OMITTED LETTERS

THE x's are to be replaced by letters, but the same letter must be retained throughout one sentence. The eight omitted letters will, when rearranged, spell a delightful season.

1. xda xs xn xtaly.
2. xan xarrie xarry xoal ?
3. xellie, xed's xearly xine.
4. xn xrab xte xn xpple.
5. xera's xery xain.
6. "xnly xur xlives," xrdered xscar.
7. xnn xnd xgnes xre xlice's xunts.
8. xed xook xom's xent.

Answer, p. 88

Red Coat Blue

by Michael G. Sanger

Long ago, in a small town with just one street, there lived a Prince who worked as a tailor. Prince Tevia had left his father's castle to seek adventure in foreign lands, but after a few weeks of seeking, ran low on money and had to find work as a tailor. The town he settled in, like other small towns throughout the countryside, suffered from a dry spell which plagued the land.

When the rain didn't fall, the ground grew dry. When the ground grew dry, the crops would die. And when the crops died, the farmers cried. And the young tailor cried too. For without their crops, the farmers had nothing to trade for pants and shirts or blouses and skirts. And when the farmers didn't trade, the tailor didn't eat.

So one morning, after sitting down to an empty breakfast table for the fifth day in a row, the tailor made up his mind. He took one long, last look around his workshop, and then quickly walked across the street to the barn where he kept his horse and cart.

"Hello, Marie," he called out to the old white mare poking her head over the wooden railing.

"Keep eating, old girl," he said softly. "We've got a long trip ahead of us, and not much to travel on."

Stroking her white mane, he led her into the harness.

"We're going to see some strange things," he whispered as he tightened the cinch around her neck.

"Nahahahahaha?" she asked.

"What will we see?" said the young man, pulling on a strand of brown hair that flopped across his forehead. "I really don't know. But if we knew what would happen, where would the fun be?"

He hopped into the seat of the cart; and with only the white shirt on his back, the brown leather pants on his legs, a sewing kit, and two silver coins in his pocket, he shook the reins and set out to explore the world.

Now, the young tailor had come from the North, so he set Marie on the road going south. He knew another village lay just two days ride down this road, but he had never been there before. So he didn't know about the brothers Red and Blue.

These two brothers owned farms just outside the next village — farms that lay across the road from each other. They were greedy, sneaky men, and never missed a chance to take advantage of a more trusting soul. And being so greedy and sneaky, they thought everybody else was just as bad as they were.

To keep anyone from ever stealing anything of his, the older brother painted everything on his farm red. His farmhouse was red, the barn where his cows slept was red, the fences around his wheat fields were red, the sacks he stored his grain in were red, and even the clothes he wore were red.

Not to be outdone, his younger brother, who lived just across the road, painted everything on his farm blue. His farmhouse was blue, his barn was blue, his fences were blue, his grain-bags were blue, and, yes, even his clothes were blue.

Thus, the brothers were known as Red and Blue.

On the second night of his journey, Tevia's cart approached the farms of brothers Red and Blue. Just as the cart passed between the two farms, a gentle breeze chased the clouds from before the moon, and in the bright moonlight the tailor saw Red's farm.

"Whoooa, Marie!" he called, pulling back on the reins. "What's this? An entire farm painted *red*?" He rubbed his eyes in disbelief. "I must be seeing things. Not having eaten in seven days is making me lose my grip. That whole farm can't be painted red."

To clear his head he turned to the other side of the road and was so surprised he nearly fell out of the cart.

"Oh no!" he cried. "What's this? Another farm, painted all *blue*? My hunger is making me see things."

To calm himself Tevia took a deep breath and smelled the scent of freshly cut grain. His mouth began to water, and his stomach began to growl. He thought of the grain being ground into flour, the flour being baked into bread, the bread being smothered in butter, and the delicious taste of it all. But just then his stomach growled extra loudly, and roused him from his dream.

"If I'm ever going to eat again," he said to himself, "I'd better do something, and fast."

He jumped out of his cart, and following his nose, climbed over the blue fence, crossed a field that had been worked with a blue plough, passed a blue trough where blue pigs were fed, and stopped beside a big blue barn. Stacked against the barn was a pile of blue bags, each one filled with grain.

"This farmer has plenty of grain," thought Tevia. "So he wouldn't mind if I buy a bag." He fished a silver coin out of his pocket and left it as payment. Then he picked up a large blue bag, and with a grunt and a heave, tossed it onto his shoulder.

It happened that the bag he picked had a small hole in one corner, and out of this tiny hole trickled a thin trail of golden grain. This trail followed Tevia past the blue trough, across the field, over the blue fence, and into the middle of the road. The trail stopped where Tevia stopped to toss the bag into his cart.

As he was about to climb into the cart and drive off, a thought came to him. "It wouldn't be neighbourly to take a bag of grain from the blue farm and not from the red one."

So he climbed over the red fence, crossed the field that had been ploughed by a red plough, passed a red trough where red pigs were fed, and stopped beside the big red barn with its pile of red grain bags. Picking out a nice looking bag, the tailor heaved it onto his shoulder, and leaving his other silver coin as payment, started back to his cart.

As luck would have it, the red bag also had a small hole in it, and it too left a thin trail of golden grain. This trail followed the tailor from the red barn, past the red trough, across the field, and over the red fence. It stopped where Tevia stopped to toss the bag into his cart, right next to the blue bag.

Short of breath, Tevia climbed into his cart and continued on towards town, where he hoped to trade some of the grain for a meal and a place to stay. The rest he planned to give to someone hungrier than himself.

As he drove away, a cloud drifted in front of the moon, but before it did an owl sitting in a tree noticed the trail of grain running from Blue's barn to Red's; or it might have been from Red's barn to Blue's. The fading moonlight made it hard to tell which.

The next morning, just as the sun peeked over the edge of the land, the brothers Red and Blue climbed out of their beds and walked sleepily towards their barns to do the morning milking. As each man approached his barn, he noticed a thin trail of golden grain leading away from his pile of bags and quickly concluded that he had been robbed.

23

The Green Tiger's Caravan

Thinking quickly, both Red and Blue grabbed pitchforks and followed the trail. They were so eager to catch the "thief" that they never even noticed the silver coins left as payment. Putting their noses to the trail, they hurried from their barns, past their troughs, across their fields, and over their fences to the middle of the road, where they bumped heads.

"Ouch!" they both yelled at the same time, rubbing their heads. "What are you doing here?"

"Somebody stole my grain," said Red, "and I'm following this trail to catch him."

"Don't try to fool me," said Blue, still rubbing his head. "I can see the trail runs up to your barn, and that means just one thing. You stole my grain."

"What?" cried Red. "I don't know what kind of trick you're trying, but it won't work. It's plain as plain can be that the trail leads to your barn, which means you're the thief."

"Me? Steal your grain? Don't make me laugh."

"Well I certainly wouldn't waste my time stealing anything from you!"

Both men raised their pitchforks, and blood would have flowed if the county judge hadn't walked by on his way to town.

"Just a minute, men!" the judge called, running up to stop the fight. "What's going on here?"

"He stole my grain," accused Red.

"Liar!" bellowed Blue. "You stole my grain, and the trail proves it." Again the brothers would have come to blows had the judge not stepped between them.

"Just a moment," said the judge. "Each of you is accusing the other of having stolen a bag of grain. And you both claim this trail of grain as your proof?"

"That's right," the brothers agreed.

"Well then, tomorrow I want to see both of you in court, where we can settle this properly. Until then, no more fighting. Understand?"

Grudgingly the brothers nodded in agreement, and walked back to their farms. The judge continued on his way.

The night before, Tevia had stopped at a small inn on the edge of town, trading some grain for a room and a hearty meal, and giving the rest to a young couple with two hungry children. He kept the bags for himself, as a reminder of the two curious farms painted entirely red and blue.

Now, as Tevia sat at a large oak table, sniffing the freshly baked bread and preparing himself for a fine breakfast, the county judge walked in. The judge was a great talker, and immediately told the innkeeper about his meeting with Red and Blue. When Tevia heard that the two brothers thought they had been robbed and were accusing each other, a smile spread across his face.

"Who do you think will win the case?" asked the innkeeper.

"I don't know," replied the judge, "and I really don't care. I hope they both lose. God knows they have more grain than they know what to do with. It isn't that the theft hurt them; it's just that they're so pigheaded."

The innkeeper nodded his head in agreement. "What those two need is someone to teach them a lesson. Someone to teach them not to be so sure they're always right."

"That's for sure," said the judge, getting up to leave. "See you in court tomorrow." And the judge left the inn, never noticing Tevia, who had been listening eagerly to all he had said and who was now boiling with anger.

He was angry, first, because the brothers were hoarding grain that hungry people needed, and, second, because in their haste to think the worst, they hadn't even noticed the silver coins he'd left as payment. He boiled for a few minutes, and then stood up, a huge grin on his

Red Coat Blue

face. He had a plan.

Running to the barn he took scissors, needles, and thread out of his sewing kit and went to work on the red and blue bags. All day long he snipped and sewed, and by nightfall he had tailored a most amazing outfit — half red, and half blue.

Trying it on, he looked at his reflection in an old mirror. It was better than perfect! When he turned his left side to the mirror, he appeared to be clothed entirely in blue. When he turned his right side to the mirror, his clothes appeared to be entirely red. Facing the mirror directly the suit was half red, half blue — divided straight down the middle.

Wearing his suit of red and blue, he climbed onto Marie's back and rode out to the brothers' farms.

When he reached the spot where he'd stopped the night before, he called out, "Red! Blue! Come to your doors. I have something to tell you."

Both brothers came to their doors, Red in a red nightshirt, Blue in a blue one. Looking out, both men saw a man sitting on a white horse. Red saw a man wearing a suit of blue while Blue saw a man dressed all in red.

"What do you want?" they yelled.

"Were you robbed last night?" asked Tevia.

"Yes," they both replied. "By my brother."

"Well, I know who took your grain and will testify in court tomorrow. The man you want is wearing a suit the same color as mine."

Since Red saw Tevia's blue side, and Blue saw his red side, each man was sure that this stranger would help him convict his brother. Tevia rode back to the inn, and the brothers went back to bed, each sure that the morrow would bring him victory.

The next morning Red and Blue woke up, put on their best clothes, and started towards town. Blue was dressed in a fine suit of royal blue; Red wore a ruby red outfit. Though they walked side by side the entire way into town, neither spoke a word to the other.

News of this case had spread throughout the village, and a large crowd was gathered in the town square which served as a courtyard. As the two brothers took their places on either end of the judge's bench, the town crier cried, "Come to order, come to order. Here comes the judge. Here comes the judge." A hush fell over the crowd as the magistrate took his place, adjusted his white wig, and said; "Let the proceedings proceed."

"Your honor," cried the crier again, "Red is claiming his brother Blue stole a bag of his grain two nights ago, and Blue is claiming the same."

"Red," said the judge. "What evidence makes you suspect your brother?"

"Your honor, not only does the trail of grain lead from my barn to his, but a witness said he saw Blue do it."

"You liar!" cried Blue. "The trail leads to your barn, and he said he saw you do it."

"He said you!"

"YOU!"

"Gentlemen, gentlemen, please," said the judge. "Where is this witness? We must have this witness."

"Here I am," said Tevia as he made his way through the crowd. He walked straight up to the judge, making sure the red side of his suit was towards Blue, and the blue side towards Red.

"That's the man," cried both brothers at the same time.

The judge smiled, and several townspeople chuckled as they saw the two-toned suit and realized what was going on.

"Your honor," said the tailor, "I can solve this case, but I require a bag of grain and one gold coin from each of the brothers for the trouble I've gone to."

While a gold coin would buy several bags of grain, the brothers were so set on convicting each other that they each agreed to pay.

"I'm the man you're looking for," Tevia began. "I took one bag from each of you, never dreaming they'd leak and leave a trail. I suggest you keep your bags in better repair from now on." He took the scissors, needles, and thread out of his pocket and gave them to Red and Blue.

"Sew up your bags so this kind of thing doesn't happen again," he suggested.

"The trails ran into each other, making it look like a single bag had been carried from one farm to the other."

"But what about last night," asked Blue. "You said Red did it."

"You said Blue did it," Red countered.

"I said the man who took the grain had the same color suit as I wore."

Only now did Tevia turn around, letting the brothers see his suit had two sides of different colors. The townspeople howled with glee while the brothers stared at the ground, wishing they could disappear.

But suddenly the brothers both looked up — triumphant grins on their faces.

"You think you're pretty smart," said Red. "But you did steal a bag or grain from each of us."

A worried hush fell across the crowd.

"I didn't steal your grain; I paid for it. Go back home, and look where the bags are missing. You'll each find a silver coin, which is more than fair payment."

The crowd hooted and whistled. The judge nodded sagely. The brothers looked like they were about to cry.

"Keep the grain," Tevia said. "Or give it to someone who needs it."

The brothers both nodded.

"I'm sorry," said Red.

"Me too," said Blue. They gave Tevia his coins and turned towards each other for the walk back home.

"Just a second," called Tevia. "Listen to this. It might help you stay out of trouble.

I showed just half my coat to each,
This simple lesson you to teach.
Share the other's point of view
And you'll have no need of Red Coat Blue."

The brothers returned home, and Tevia, after being treated to a fine meal, hitched Marie to the cart and continued on his way. The brothers Red and Blue never saw him again.

Push My Go Button

by F. J. Bursten

It was one of those days. Lenny woke up mad. He didn't want to dress. He didn't want to play. He didn't want to eat. He didn't feed the dog. He kicked the cat. He pushed his sister off her chair.

At last Mother said, "Go to your room and stay there."

Lenny went to his room. Now he was *really* mad.

"No one likes me," he said to himself. "I'll run away. That's what I'll do. Run away. Then they will all miss me. They will all wish I was here. I'll go far away. I won't come back for a long time."

Lenny dressed to go outdoors. He looked for money. There were no pennies in his pockets. There was no money in his room.

"Oh, well!" he said to himself. "Who needs money? I will ask for anything I need."

Lenny went out the back way. No one saw him go.

He went down to the corner. A truck came by. Lenny waved. The truck stopped. The man in the truck said, "Can I help you?"

"I need a ride," said Lenny. "Where are you going?"

"I'm going downtown," said the man.

"No," said Lenny. "That is not very far. I want to be gone a long time. A long, long time. Thank you anyway. Goodbye."

The man shook his head. The truck went on.

Lenny went down the block. There was a bench there. He sat down. A bus came by. It stopped.

"Get in," said the bus driver. "Where are you going?"

"I don't know," said Lenny. "Where are *you* going?"

"I'm going to the other side of town," said the bus driver. "Do you want to get in? Or *don't* you want to get in?" "No, I don't," said Lenny. "That is not far. I want to be gone a long time. A long, long time! Thank you anyway. Goodbye."

The bus driver shook his head. The bus went on.

Lenny walked some more. He came to the park. No one was in the park. Children were home, looking at TV cartoons. Fathers and mothers were working. No one was in the park.

Lenny say down under a tree. "This is no fun," he said to himself. "I am not far away yet. It is not a long time yet. I am tired. I want to go home. But it is too soon to go home. No one will miss me yet. I will just have to stay here some more. I will play by myself."

Lenny went to the swings. He had to go by some little green trees. Something moved in the trees. Lenny stopped to look. He saw a little green face. Then a little man stepped out. He was all green. He was dressed in green too.

"Hello!" said Lenny.

The little green man pushed a button on his chest. Then he said "Hello!" too. It sounded funny to Lenny.

"Want to play?" asked Lenny. "Let's go swing."

He ran to the swings. The little green man ran too.

The Green Tiger's Caravan

They played on the swings. They played on other things too. They played and played. They were tired. They sat down.

"I have to go now," said the little green man. "I have been gone a long time. I ran away from home. I wanted them to miss me. Now I am going back."

"Where do you live?" asked Lenny.

"On the other side of your stars," said the little green man. "It is far, far away. Do you want to come with me? My friends will like you."

Lenny said to himself, "Good! He lives far, far away. It will take a long time to get there. It will take a long time to get back. Just what I want!"

Lenny said to the little green man, "Yes, I will go with you. But I do not have a ship. I do not have a rocket. How will I get back home?"

"Oh, I do not have a ship," said the little green man. "I do not have a rocket. I do not need one. See my buttons? This one says GO. If I push it, I will go. First I think of some place. Then I push my GO button. And I am there! You can come back any time you want. Just push this button. Think of where to go. That's all! You won't be there. You will be here."

"That's bad," said Lenny to himself. "It will not take long to get there. It will not take long to get back. Mother will not miss me. I will have to *stay* there a long time. Then she will miss me. Yes, I will play there a long time." Lenny said to the little green man, "All right! Let's go."

"Hold my hand," said the little green man. "I will push the buttom. We will be there now. Give me your hand."

The little green man held Lenny's hand. He pushed his GO button. Then he let go of Lenny's hand.

They were in a little green house. There were other little green men there. They all had little green buttons on their chests. They were glad to see Lenny's friend. They looked at Lenny.

"Look what I have!" said the little green man.

"An earth man!" said the other little green men. "How cute! Can he do tricks? Can he sing? Does he make smoke? Can he dance? Show us, earth man!"

"Don't tease him," said the little green man. "He is smart. He is good at playing. He is as good as we are. He can swing. He can see-saw. He can slide. He is not my pet. He is my friend. He came to see us. He has to go home soon. Let's show him our town first."

All the little green men held hands. Lenny held hands with them. Then one pushed his GO button.

They were downtown. All the people on the street were green. All the stores were green. And all the things in the stores were green.

"Time to play, now!" said one of the little green men. "He said you were a good player. Come with us! We will see how good you are!"

"Yes! Yes!" said the other little green men. "We want to play now. Let's all go to the air park."

One of the little green men pushed his GO button. They were all in an air park. Little green men were playing there. They swung in the air. They dived and turned in the air. They jumped up and down in the air. Lenny and his new friends played a long, long time. Lenny was playing with them all the time. He held hands and played in the air too. Then he let go.

Down he fell! It did not hurt much. But his pants were all green where he fell in the green dirt.

The little green men picked him up. "We played too hard," they said. "We forgot that you were an earth man. You played just like we did. You are a good player!"

28

Push My Go Button

"I think it is time for me to go," said Lenny. "I have been here a long time. They will be missing me at home. They will want me back now."

"I will look for you in the park next time when I come," said the little green man. "You are fun to play with. But you have *not* been gone long. Our time goes backwards. It is not like your time. You will see what I mean when you get home."

"I don't understand you," said Lenny.

"You will," said the little green man. "Here — think of where you want to go. Now — push my GO button. Goodbye."

Lenny did not want to go back to the park. He was too tired to walk anymore. So he wished to be back home. Back home, in his own room. He pushed the GO button. And there he was!

Just then his mother came in. She smiled at him. "That was fast!" she said. "You got dressed right away. You must be feeling better. You have only been here a little while. Do you want to eat now? When you are done, you can go to play next door. Davie wants you to come. But put on other pants. These pants have green dirt on them. Where on earth did you get that kind of dirt?"

Lenny just smiled at his mother. "I don't know where they got dirty," he said. "I really don't."

"Well," said Mother, "no story is better than a silly story. I'm glad you didn't tell me that you didn't get the dirt *anywhere* on earth! Put the dirty pants on top of the washer. Then come and eat. It is still morning. You can have a long, long time to play today."

Mother smiled and went out. Lenny smiled at himself. Time that ran backwards was a good, good time. He took off his dirty pants. He put on clean pants. Then he pushed a button on his shirt.

"Zoom!" he said. "Food, here I come!"

Then Lenny ran out of the room.

BEHEADINGS
To Behead a word, cut off its first letter like this—

BEHEAD A TOY AND LEAVE EVERY BIT. THE TOY IS A BALL. CUT OFF THE FIRST LETTER AND LEAVE ALL.

1.

I tell the time: behead me and I fasten the door.

2.

Behead a part of your book and leave old.

3.

Behead what you wear on your foot and leave what you use in your garden.

4.

Behead cold and leave high ground: behead again and leave sick.

Answers, p. 88

Surprise on the Beach

by Virginia Castello

The month was July, time for summer's fun at the rented cottage near the ocean. Larry Jenkins waited excitedly all winter for this month to come. He loved the smell of the ocean breeze. He wanted to find treasures on the beach. And, best of all, he enjoyed the wonderful sense of aloneness away from the big city, away from the busy world. He couldn't wait to get started.

Larry rolled his blue jeans up to his knees. He donned a wide-brimmed, straw hat and sunk both hands deeply into his pockets. Then, the young boy began to explore the water's edge. Down, down the beach he walked, kicking the sand aside with his feet. Suddenly, he paused, peering hard at something strange in the distance. It appeared to be a bird. Yes, it was a bird. But it wasn't moving. It remained very still. This puzzled Larry very much. So, he began to walk faster and faster, until he found himself running towards the still and quiet bird. He could make out the markings now — light, pearl-grey feathers with a white tail and throat, about fifteen inches long.

Coming up alongside, Larry looked up at the sea gull and exclaimed loudly, "Why, you're a wooden bird! That's why you've been so still!" Elated over his discovery, Larry sat himself at the bottom of the post upon which the bird perched, covering both of his feet with the soft and silky sand. Looking upward, he eyed the bird with boyish curiosity. "I bet you've been here a long time. Your color is all faded and your feathers are all chipped and peeled."

It was true. The wooden bird had been perched upon the wooden post for a long, long time. And the salty air had chipped and faded his feathers. Larry continued to speak to the bird as the foamy waves gently brushed the tips of his toes. "Gosh, look at that water! It just seems to go on and on, without any end. I bet you get pretty lonely out here, Mister Bird." Looking up at his wooden friend, Larry eagerly asked, "Do you want me to be your friend, Mister Bird?"

At that very moment, Larry put his hand up to the bird's cheek. "Why, that's a tear drop on your face! Mister Bird ... you're crying!" Larry reached out to his friend. "Don't cry, Mister Bird. I'd love to be your friend." He continued excitedly, "I've got a great idea! Tomorrow, I'll come back with some fresh paint and I'll paint you like new, again. Yep, I'll fix you up real nice."

On the following day, Larry returned with some fresh paint and a new paint brush. And, within a few hours, Mister Bird glistened proudly under the bright sun. "Gosh!" Larry exclaimed. "You look really beautiful, Mister Bird, really and truly beautiful!"

Each day, Larry came to visit his friend. Each day, they watched the different ships out at sea. Sometimes, they talked about sunken ships and treasures of the deep and exchanged stories about pirates of yesteryear. Each day was an exciting day. Yet, Larry seemed to be upset about something.

He began slowly. "Mister Bird, you're my friend, and I wouldn't want to say anything to spoil that. But, there's something missing ... What I'm trying to say, Mister Bird, is that I wish you could fly. Oh, I wish you could fly."

As Larry was speaking, a strange, crunching sound filled the air. Larry stood with his mouth wide open. "Wow!" he yelled. "You broke free from your post! Mister Bird, you can fly!"

Together, they roamed the sandy beach. Sometimes, Larry picked up flat stones and sent them spinning out to sea. Sometimes, they stopped to admire the beautiful shells along the way. And at other times, they sailed into the wind, until Larry collapsed laughingly upon the sand while Mister Bird perched upon his nose. There was so much to see and so much to do.

They were so happy ... until that final day when Larry came to tell his friend goodbye. "Mister Bird, I won't be able to see you anymore. We're going back to the city today."

"Don't feel sad," Mister Bird chirped. "Just think of what we can do next year!"

"I know," answered Larry, sadly. "I just didn't want it to end. And I'll never find another friend like you. Will you wait for me, Mister Bird ... I mean, really wait for me?"

Mister Bird flapped his wings happily. "I'll be here, my friend, right here on this post, just where you found me."

Larry smiled and reached out to pet his friend. He stroked his wooden, light pearl-grey feathers. He stroked his wooden, white tail and throat. He murmured quietly, "Goodbye, Mister Bird. Goodbye, my friend," as he gently wiped a tear from the proud bird's eye.

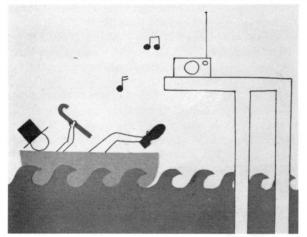

IF YOU SCRAMBLE
A DANCING SHOE
AND A DIVING BOARD. .
WHAT DO YOU HAVE?

DANCING BOARDS
AND A DIVING SHOE.

31

The Crying Dolls

Adapted from the Hungarian of Jeno J. Tersanszky
by Theodore and Helen Benedek Schoenman
Illustrated by Nancie West Swanberg

Once upon a time there was a woman who had two daughters. One of them was her own and the other a stepdaughter. Her own child she pampered and spoiled. She dressed her in fine clothes and spared her from work. She did exactly the opposite with her poor step-daughter. She had to do all the hard work around the house. She went around in rags and was scolded, harassed, and beaten day in and day out by her cruel stepmother.

One day the woman was going to a party with her daughter whom she had dressed up like a Christmas tree. The girl's suitor accompanied them to the party. While they were away, the stepdaughter had to stay home to watch the house. To make sure that she should not be idle, the stepmother had pressed on her a bundle of used clothes to mend.

The poor girl was not only diligent but also very skillful with her hands. She quickly got through with the vast amount of work. Then, instead of thinking to take a rest, she thought of amusing herself a little. All around, there were a lot of rags on the floor — remnants of her mending, ready to be swept out.

"I know! I'll make a doll out of these," thought the little girl. With that she began the new and pleasant task. First, she made the doll's head. She wanted to make it a laughing one. Let at least her doll be as happy as she was miserable. It was a great success. She was very pleased with the doll's grinning face. Happily, feverishly, she stitched together the many colorful rags. Quickly, she formed the shape of the doll, completely absorbed in her work.

When she finished the last stitches, she picked up the beautiful doll and held it high to better inspect it. The doll looked at her in such a sweetly odd, laughing way that a loud, heartfelt laugh burst out of the little girl.

At that moment the door opened and in stormed the wicked stepmother. "So! You are wasting your time with such worthless trifles? You hideous frog, you!" she screamed at the frightened little girl. "Are you beginning to play with dolls? You lazy good-for-nothing."

She tore the doll out of the little girl's hand and threw it out the window. Then she fell on her poor stepdaughter and beat her mercilessly.

The little girl cried bitterly. But, what hurt her more than the beating was that the wicked stepmother took the beautiful laughing doll, which she had made with such great care, and threw it out.

The suitor of the other girl was also present at this ugly family squabble, for, following the dictate of propriety, he had escorted home the mother and daughter. He felt sorry for the poor little stepdaughter; but, of course, he could not interfere in the affairs of a strange family.

As he took his leave and went through the gate into the street, he noticed the doll lying in the dust. He picked it up and took it with him. It was his intention to secretly return it to the little girl. It was nighttime and dark. The young man did not look at the doll; he just stuck it in his coat pocket and forgot about it.

And so it happened that the next day, when the young man went to the market, he had the doll in his pocket. As he was dawdling about, looking at the many different things for sale, he

32

The Crying Dolls

blinded from all the sewing. Her back hurt and the tips of her fingers were all bloody. She stuck herself many times in her haste. And as though this were not enough, the stepmother stood behind her, striking her with a switch for not working fast enough. So the only joy in the little girl's miserable life turned into accursed suffering. What could be worse than that?

After the wicked woman had accumulated a large number of dolls, she decided to take the whole lot of them to the market. Greedily, she dreamt of all the money she would get for the dolls. A wagon transported them to the fair, and a large tent was put up in which to exhibit them.

But what is this? What happened? People completely ignored them. And that was better than when they glanced at them. Startled, they would turn their eyes away. They grimaced, they cursed and, uttering disparaging remarks, they went on, giving a wide berth to the stepmother's tent.

The angry and bewildered stepmother nearly burst with rage in her bitter disappointment. After all, the dolls were exactly like the first and the second one. And looking at those, people teetered in their mirth. The wicked woman could not understand the reason for the people's behaviour.

Finally, in a loud voice, she started to call the customers to the dolls.

"Now, really, dear friends! How is it that you are not casting your eyes on my dolls and no longer laugh at them, as before? Just see how sweetly my dolls smile at you."

"Smile, eh?" spoke a man from the crowd, and others agreed with his words. "Laugh, eh? Perhaps you have lost your reason, you old witch. The dolls are crying and one gets only soured and depressed looking at them."

Yes! That is exactly what happened. The first of the dolls, which the little girl made with joy, incited laughter with their grinning countenance. The other dolls, made in her misery, saddened the people. After all, the twist of the mouth and the lines of the face are similar whether one laughs or cries. It is hard to tell how the expression of joy turned into pain in the grimace of the dolls.

Oh! The wicked stepmother nearly had a stroke in her raging fury. On whom would she take out her rage?

She attacked her daughter's suitor, for he was the one who got her into this. He had persuaded her to have the stepdaughter make all the dolls, and now she was stuck with them. And all the money she spent in their making was lost. With foul curses she reviled the young man.

In vulgar language he could not compete with his prospective mother-in-law, but he revenged himself in other ways.

He went to the poor little stepdaughter (instead of the lazy and tawdry daughter) and asked her to marry him. It was certainly much better for him in marrying this hardworking girl with her faithful heart.

The Razzle-Dazzle Circus

by Vicki J. Althoff

The Razzle-Dazzle Circus Train
Chugged into Feelin' Flats.
The steamy engine wiped her brow
And rested on her tracks.

The Elegants in proud array
Paraded down the ramp;
The roustarounds unpacked the poles,
Began to set up camp.

Soon children of the dreary burg
Had gathered all around.
Eyes wide, they watched the red-striped tent
Unrolled upon the ground.

The tamer got the thions out.
(They walk upon their thighs.)
And exercised them in the yard
Before excited eyes.

The Forces reared and plunged and danced;
They went through all their paces.
Frown stealers put red noses on
Then whitened up their faces.

By noon the great Parade began:
Performers dressed in spangles
Prepared to ride into the town
on Elegants and Girangles.

The Acromen turned floppy flips,
Lapease artistes performed
Atop a wagon strung with wires
And pulled by two Shirorm.

In cages, all the Thions paced,
And, right on cue, they roared,
While fascinated townsmen stopped
And Flattened feelings soared.

The Mayor and Council at Town Hall
Declared a "Circus Day."
And people gathered at the tent
Their faces bright and gay.

They watched the walkers on the wires
And clapped their hands with glee,
To see Fleals juggle with their snouts
And watch the dancing Brie.

For Feelin' Flats was feelin' good
To laugh and dance and play.
The Mayor stood up to make a speech.
He said, "Please, won't you stay?"

The Circus Master tipped his hat
And made a little bow.
"I thank you, sir, but we must go
To other places, now.

For there are many towns like yours
That need a bit of fun;
We have to spread our joy around.
Tomorrow, we must run."

By early morn the show was packed
Inside the train car walls.
That night they livened up more hearts
In sad old Moody Falls.

Martin and the Popcorn Snow

by Jan Thomas
illustrated by Joyce Eide

This is Martin. He lives with his mom and dad and his big sister, Jill. Noodles is Martin's very own cat.

One cold night in January something very, very strange happened, but only Martin remembers it. Martin was in his pajamas and stood looking out the window. It was late that night and the moon was shining brightly when the strange thing happened.

At first Martin thought it was snowing, but the snow flakes looked too big and round. He pressed his nose against the frosted window and stared hard. It couldn't be! It was snowing popcorn!

Imagine that! Snowing popcorn. Martin raced downstairs to tell his family.

"Dad, Dad, it's snowing popcorn," said Martin.

"Mmm hmm," replied his father.

"Mother, it really is. It's snowing popcorn outside."

"Yes, dear. Go brush your teeth," said his mother.

Martin ran back upstairs and brushed his teeth a little, but he was so excited he forgot to put any toothpaste on his toothbrush. When he looked out the bathroom window, it was still coming down. Popcorn *was* falling from the sky.

"Jill, Jill, it's snowing popcorn. There is popcorn everywhere!"

"Go away, Martin. Can't you see I'm on the phone," Jill said.

Martin went to his bedroom. No one believed him. He looked out the window again. Now there were big piles of popcorn everywhere. There were mounds of it. There were hills of it!

More and more popcorn fell from the sky. The bushes were covered with it. Popcorn hung all over the trees. The telephone wires were white with popcorn. Mrs. Jenkin's car was buried in popcorn. It was all over their porch and in their driveway. Every roof top, garbage can, street sign, dog house, sand box, and swing set on the block wore a coat of popcorn.

Martin opened his window just a crack. There it was, right on his window sill. He grabbed a handful and popped it into his mouth. It *was* popcorn and it was warm! It smelled wonderful! Martin hadn't even thought about it being warm.

Martin couldn't wait any longer. Quietly he tip-toed down the stairs, through the hall, past the living room, past his mother and father, past the dining room, through the kitchen, to the back door. Carefully, quietly he put on his boots, his coat, his hat and mittens. He opened the door very, very slowly. He hoped that it wouldn't creak. Martin stepped outside and then slowly, quietly, carefully shut the door.

He ran off, knee-high in popcorn. Martin laughed. He jumped up and down and shouted. He opened his mouth and caught popcorn on his tongue, and then he lay down and rolled in it. What fun! It tasted so good that he ate it by the handful.

Then Martin heard the noise of an engine. He looked down the street and saw two big trucks. They were moving slowly. The first truck had "CITY" printed on the side of it. As it drove past, Martin saw the word "SALT" printed on the back. Why, the city was salting all the popcorn!

The second truck looked like a fire engine. It had hoses and a flashing light, but it wasn't red. It was yellow! A man stood on the back of the truck with a hose. He smiled and waved at Martin. Suddenly Martin realized what kind of truck it was. It was a butter truck with real butter spouting from the hose!

It is very strange to snow popcorn. It is even stranger to snow warm popcorn. But Martin could not even imagine having warm, buttered, salted popcorn everywhere. Salt and butter trucks, how wonderful!

Martin began throwing it in the air. He danced around and jumped up and down. He giggled.

"This is great!" shouted Martin. "I love popcorn."

Martin decided to fill his wagon with popcorn. He ran and pulled it out of the garage. Then he found a pail and shovel buried beneath the popcorn in his sandbox. He scooped and scooped until the little red wagon was full. Martin was getting full, too, because after every scoop he put in the wagon, he ate a scoop.

But what if all the popcorn on the ground melted? "I must have more," Martin thought. "I must save it." So he started to fill everything he could find.

Martin dragged buckets and boxes and old flower pots from the garage. He filled his dad's wheelbarrow and tool chest. He even emptied the garbage cans and filled them. Martin filled himself, too. He ate and he ate and he ate. Martin loved popcorn.

It was getting very late. Martin had scooped and scooped, filling everything he could think of. He was very tired and very, very full. He had eaten at least one hill of popcorn all by himself!

"Ohhhhhh, ohhh," Martin moaned. He rolled over. Suddenly all the white popcorn covered him. It was very smooth. The white popcorn became his white blanket. Martin opened his eyes wide. He was in his bed in his own bedroom! It was the middle of the night and Martin realized he had been dreaming. All that popcorn, all that delicious, warm, salted, buttered popcorn had just been a dream. He sighed and pulled the blanket up around him. As he turned over, Martin glanced out the window. It was snowing.

Wilbur

by Jim Latimer

There once was a rabbit named Wilbur who was exceptionally brown. As brown as cinnamon or whole wheat. As brown as butterscotch. Or March maple. As brown as these and browner still. He was glistening, gladdening, heartbreaking brown. He was astonishingly brown. Exceptionally brown. Though almost no one ever noticed.

Once Wilbur was walking in the woods, watching for clover, not watching where he was going. He ran — CRASH — into a fox.

The fox, startled, shouted, "RECKLESS RABBIT. WATCH WHERE YOU'RE GOING. THIS IS A FOX." The fox thought about it. "I am a fox," he said. "Foxes are FIERCE toward rabbits." The more the fox thought the more furious and indignant he became. "I HAVE HALF A MIND TO EAT YOU," he shouted fiercely. "No, I have a WHOLE MIND to eat you. Prepare yourself, rabbit, to be eaten."

Wilbur looked at the fox with calm eyes. "I don't know whether you noticed, fox," he said, "But I am very brown. My name is Wilbur."

The fox looked at Wilbur, suddenly noticing. This rabbit *was* exceptionally brown. As brown as cinnamon or whole wheat. As brown as butterscotch and browner still. The fox's eyes grew wide. He gasped. Wilbur was such a glossy, beautiful brown the fox felt glad and heartbroken both at once. He rose up on tiptoe and began to dance, capering and trotting. The fox danced around Wilbur in a wide circle, then swept up to him and gave him a hug. "You are *exceptionally* brown," he said, suddenly bursting into tears.

Wilbur patted the fox and thanked him for his generous words. They shook paws.

The fox dropped onto all fours and gamboled into the woods. "If you are ever in trouble," he said over his shoulder, "Just woof once like a fox."

"All right," said Wilbur. "If *you're* ever in trouble, just shout WILBUR."

The fox disappeared. Wilbur continued, pursuing his way, watching for clover and green plants, not watching where he was going. He ran — BANG — into a badger.

"RECKLESS RABBIT, THIS IS A BADGER," the badger shouted. This badger had never been banged by a rabbit. He was furious with indignation and injured pride. "Badgers don't eat rabbits," he said fiercely, "But they bite them. I have half — no — I have a WHOLE MIND to bite you. Prepare yourself to be bitten, rabbit."

Wilbur looked at the badger calmly. "I don't know whether you noticed, badger," he said, "But I am very brown. My name is Wilbur."

The badger looked at Wilbur, suddenly noticing. This rabbit was exceptionally brown. As brown as cinnamon or butterscotch and browner still. The badger gasped, feeling gladdened and heartbroken both at once. He wanted to dance on tiptoe, but knew his toes wouldn't support his ungainly badger's bulk. The badger turned a somersault and jumped (not very high) for joy. Giving Wilbur a hug, he burst into tears. "You are beautiful," he said. "Exceptional."

Wilbur patted the badger's back, thanked him and they shook paws.

The badger dropped to all fours and gamboled into the woods. "If you're ever in trouble," he said over his shoulder, "Just woof once like a badger."

"All right," said Wilbur. "If *you* are ever in trouble, just shout WILBUR."

The badger disappeared and Wilbur resumed his way, watching for clover and sweet grass, not watching where he was going. He ran — BOOM — into a bear.

The bear looked at Wilbur. "Rabbit?" he said, not quite seeing (bears have dim eyesight). But this *was* a rabbit — his nose told him. "Do rabbits run into bears?" the bear wondered. "Do rabbits *boom* bears?" The more the bear thought, the more resentful he decided to be. "Bears are not normally fierce toward rabbits," he said aloud, "But I feel I am going to be fierce toward *this* rabbit."

Wilbur interrupted the bear. "I don't know whether you noticed, bear," he said, "But I am very brown. My name is Wilbur."

The bear squinted. This rabbit *was* very brown. He smelt brown — as brown as butterscotch or March maple. The bear felt both glad and heartbroken. He went up on tiptoe, not remembering his toes could never support his great bear's bulk. He took one faltering, capering step, then toppled in a heap. He tried to somersault, but he was too fat to tuck his head between his paws. Sighing, the bear turned around three times in place and gave Wilbur a hug, a tear wetting the whiskers around his eyes. "Wonderful rabbit," he said.

Wilbur patted the bear, thanked him and they shook paws. "If you ever need a rabbit, just shout WILBUR," he said.

The bear shuffled into the woods. "If you ever need a bear," he called over his shoulder, "Just woof."

When Wilbur got home, his mother was cross. "You're late," she said, looking at him closely. "You've been keeping company with bears. And badgers. (She looked at him very closely). And foxes," she added. She was hard to fool. "Well, you're not to go into the Left Side of the forest hereafter, because the Lucious Flammicus is back. Everyone says so."

The Lucious Flammicus ws a very fierce animal that sometimes haunted the Left Side of the forest, so everyone said. Wilbur had never seen the Lucious Flammicus, but it was said to have the brow and back of a rhinocerous, the hair and hide of a cat. It had a rooster's comb and wattles, four mismatched hoofs, and a ghastly chicken's stomach.

On the very next occasion, Wilbur, without meaning to, strayed into the Left Side of the forest. He was watching for grass and green plants, not watching where he was going. He ran into something. Something with a cat's hair and hide. Something with four mismatched hoofs.

The Flammicus looked at Wilbur with an expression of contempt and then rich amusement. "A rabbit, is it?" it said. "A reckless rabbit, I should think." The Flammicus laughed a laugh in which contempt and amusement were equally mingled.

Its hoofs *were* mismatched, Wilbur saw. There was one goat's hoof, one buffalo's hoof, one unicorn's hoof and one — (Wilbur couldn't make out what its fourth hoof was. An armadillo's hoof? Wilbur wondered. Do armadillos *have* hoofs?)

The Flammicus had a rhinocerous' forehead. Its wattles shivered horribly when it laughed. Its chicken's stomach was ghastly.

Wilbur shuddered. He felt his fur grow suddenly dim.

"Let's see," said the Flammicus, considering idly what might be a response appropriate to Wilbur's breach of conduct — to his unmistakable indiscretion. "Let's see," he repeated aloud. "How does a Flammicus respond, typically, to a rabbit? As a rule, Flammicuses are not fierce to rabbits. We don't eat them, I shouldn't think. But we sometimes KILL them." The Flammicus' wattles shivered.

"I don't know whether you noticed, Flammicus, but I am very brown," Wilbur said feebly, hoping he still was.

41

"I noticed," said the Flammicus, "But I don't know why you bring it up — your being brown, I mean. It's not relevant, don't you see? It's not pertinent." The Flammicus searched for an expression better suited to its meaning. "It's not helpful, not *useful* in the present circumstances. Now, if you will just step forward. That's right. And I'll just trouble you to count — you don't mind counting with me, do you? — and we'll have done with you on the count of three."

Wilbur woofed.

"Dear, dear." The Flammicus clucked and shook its wattles. "I'm afraid woofing (That was a woof, wasn't it? A fox's woof, I thought.) — I'm afraid a fox woof is no use." The Flammicus counted *one*.

Wilbur woofed again.

"Dear, dear," the Flammicus said again. "What was that? A badger's woof? I'm afraid a badger's woof is no use either." The Flammicus resumed counting, "Two."

Wilbur woofed like a bear.

The Flammicus shook its head sadly. It was coming to like this rabbit in a way, coming to admire his courage. The Flammicus almost wished it was not compelled to kill him. But it had committed itself, and for a Flammicus a commitment is binding. It counted *three*.

At the count of three, sensing something strangely amiss, the Flammicus suddenly looked about. It was surrounded by three very fierce, very disapproving-looking animals. One was a fox. One was a badger. One was a bear. The fox woofed — a sharp shearing woof: so sharp it sheared leaves from trees. The badger woofed — such a bleak bark it blunted nettles in the fields. The bear woofed — such a dreadful, deafening woof it dismantled spiders' webs. It turned moths into caterpillars.

The Flammicus' wattles shivered. Its rhinocerous brow beaded with perspiration. "Well," it said meekly, stalling for time, "Well, if you like to put it that way, I see what you mean. I think I quite agree with you." The Flammicus reared back suddenly on its armadillo hoof and goat-galloped away, lurching ludicrously on its left buffalo leg.

Meanwhile, Wilbur, the fox, the badger and the bear shook paws. "Well met, and good riddance," they said.

The three predators gave Wilbur a salute, then proceeded into the woods together. "*Isn't he brown?*" said the fox.

"Yes," said the badger.

"Wonderful," said the bear.

Wilbur gazed after them, blinking, drying the damp fur around his eyes with his paw. The fox, the badger and the bear were his friends for life, and the Lucious Flammicus was not seen in the Left Side of the forest again.

THE THREE RABBITS

Draw three rabbits, so that each shall appear to have two **ears,** while, in fact, they have only three ears between them.

Answer, p. 88

The Labyrinth

by Richard Cumbie
illustrated by Scott Rogers

Giovanni lived in a little crooked house across the street from the old Roman Coliseum. Every afternoon he skipped across the cobblestones, turned the corner, looked both ways to make sure no one was watching, then slipped into a secret passageway; it led him through a very dark tunnel and up a stone staircase to the upper levels of the Coliseum to where his friend Bruno fed the wild cats that lived there. And one sunny afternoon, as he fed fish heads to the cats, Bruno told Giovanni a story.

"These cats belong to the Kingdom of Cats," said the old man. "They are the servants of larger cats that live in the maze of rooms and corridors and passageways below ground. Every morning, just before the sun rises, I go down into the labyrinth to feed them."

"How many cats live down there?" Giovanni asked.

"Ten," the old man replied. "They are called the Leaders."

"May I go with you?"

Bruno thought for a moment. Then he said, "On one condition: you must promise never to tell anyone."

Of course, Giovanni promised.

Early the next morning, before his mother and father woke up, Giovanni slipped out of bed, got dressed, and ran across the cobblestones to meet Bruno. Soon the adventure began. They tip-toed down the stone steps that led to the labyrinth below the ground. Bruno had been there so many times that he hardly needed his flashlight to guide him through the maze of dark rooms and corridors that twisted and snaked every which-a-way. As they walked deeper and deeper into the darkness, Bruno warned Giovanni that the labyrinth was a dangerous maze where a little boy could disappear forever if he lost his way. No one was allowed to come here — no one except for Bruno.

Soon they came to a room that was filled with straw. Giovanni could not see the cats, but he could see their eyes peering at him out of the darkness.

"This is where the Leaders live, but they are afraid to come out because they do not know you. So we will just leave their food on the floor and go back."

As they were leaving the labyrinth, Bruno told Giovanni about a very special cat that lived there.

"There is one cat who is King of all the other cats. I have never seen him, but I have seen his paw print, and it's as big as a lion's paw. One day I know the King will be waiting for me."

"How do you know?" the boy asked.

"The Leaders have told me. As soon as the King is ready, he will call for me, and I will go because I am his servant, just as the little cats are the servants for the Leaders."

"What will happen when you meet the King?" Giovanni asked.

The old man's eyes sparkled in the darkness, and a faint smile turned up the corners of his mouth. "My life will be fulfilled," he replied.

When they stepped outside, the early morning light blinded them as it does people who have been lost in a cave. Giovanni was stunned by it and by the sound of people stirring to

The Labyrinth

life. He smelled sausage cooking in his mother's kitchen across the street. After saying goodbye to Bruno, he ran home to eat breakfast because his secret adventure had made him hungry.

That very same afternoon, when he went to meet Bruno, he was told something extraordinary.

"Tomorrow's the day," whispered the old man.

"For meeting the King of Cats?" Giovanni asked.

Bruno's eyes twinkled. He nodded his head.

"But how do you know?" the boy asked. He was afraid something might happen to his friend if the King of Cats was really as big as a lion. "Did one of the Leaders come and tell you?"

"It's a secret, my little friend, which I cannot reveal. Just believe me," Bruno replied. "Tomorrow's the day."

"Will you meet me afterwards and tell me what happened?" the boy asked.

Bruno did not answer at first. He looked as though he were day-dreaming. Then, he turned and hugged Giovanni and whispered in his ear. "Of course. You're the only one who will share my secret."

That night Giovanni had trouble falling asleep. He was excited and worried about Bruno. And the next morning he overslept, leaving barely enough time to eat his mother's breakfast before rushing off to school. When the last bell rang, he ran straight to the Coliseum and waited and waited and waited, but Bruno did not come to meet him as he had promised.

Giovanni was afraid that something terrible had happened down in the labyrinth. After giving the situation some careful thought, he decided to go to the police station and ask for help.

At the police station, Giovanni had to stand on his tiptoes to peer over the tall desk at the huge policeman who was shuffling some papers.

"What can I do for you?" the man asked without looking at the little boy.

"I've lost my friend," Giovanni answered bashfully. The policeman looked straight at him. "What I really mean is that my friend is lost."

"Where?" he asked.

"In the labyrinth at the Coliseum," the boy answered.

Giovanni wanted to tell the policeman about the King of Cats, but he had promised Bruno that he would never tell anyone.

"Hm..." the policeman said as he put on his hat. "Let's go see if we can find him."

Soon the policeman and Giovanni walked down the stone steps and began searching through the dark rooms and hallways for Bruno. They called his name time after time, but only the sound of "Bruno" echoing off the stone walls answered them. Twice they lost their way in the maze of rooms and corridors and were brought back to their starting point as though there was no beginning or end to the circle.

On the third try, however, they discovered a small doorway which led them down a very dark corridor that connected to another maze of rooms and hallways. Giovanni recognized this passageway from his adventure with Bruno. Soon they discovered the old man's footprints. They followed the trail that zigzagged through rooms and hallways until they came to the room where the Leaders lived. There, in the middle of the floor, was Bruno's canvas bag that he used to carry the fish heads to the Leaders. The bag was empty and none of the Leaders were in the room.

The policeman shone his light across the floor and walls, but Bruno was not there. And it

45

The Green Tiger's Caravan

appeared as though the only doorway to the room was the one from which the policeman and Giovanni had entered.

"That's strange," the policeman said, scratching his head. "Where could he have gone? His footprints lead into this room, and then they stop as though he disappeared into the walls."

"Come here quickly!" Giovanni shouted from the other side of the room. "Look what I found!"

The policeman shone his light on the floor where Giovanni was pointing. There was a huge paw print in the dirt. It was as big as a lion's paw, just as Bruno had said. Giovanni and the policeman stared at each other in astonishment.

"Look!" the boy shouted again. "Here's another..."

"And another," the policeman chimed in.

"And Bruno's footprints right next to them," Giovanni said.

They followed the tracks across the room until they bumped into a blank wall made of stone.

"That's impossible!" the policeman declared. "How in the world can anyone walk through a blank wall?" He scratched his head. "I've got an idea. You stay here and tap on the wall while I inspect the hallway for a trap door that leads to the other side. When I find the door I will walk along the other side of the wall until I come to the place where I hear you tapping."

So Giovanni began tapping his fingers on the wall. All of a sudden a door opened, and a long dark hallway stood before him. When he stepped inside the door slammed shut.

There was a very small patch of light at the end of the passageway, so Giovanni started walking towards it. As he walked, he had the feeling that he was being led deeper and deeper into the earth. There were no doors or rooms or hallways leading from the tunnel. It was as though the labyrinth above, the maze of rooms and corridors in the belly of the old Coliseum, were built especially to conceal this one secret passageway.

As he walked the patch of light grew larger, and the larger it grew the faster he walked until he stepped out into the bright sunshine. For a moment he could not see clearly because his eyes had not adjusted to the sunlight. Then he realized that he had stepped into the Kingdom of Cats. It was a strange place, indeed. The air smelled minty because catnip plants with large flowers grew wild. There were many trees with red balls of yarn dangling from the branches like apples. And there was a river nearby where colorful rainbow trout leaped from the water high into the air and cats leaned dangerously far over the water to catch the fish.

There were cats everywhere. Giovanni never dreamt there could be so many kinds of cats. There were calicos, angoras and siamese; there were toms and bobcats; there were cougars, leopards and tigers. And sitting high on a rock overlooking the Kingdom of Cats was a huge lion with a beautiful golden mane.

"That must be the King of the Kingdom of Cats," Giovanni muttered as he tiptoed backwards towards the passageway. He was very frightened.

"Don't be afraid, Giovanni."

The little boy could not believe his ears. He turned around. Bruno was standing beside a tree where mice hung from their tails.

"Will the lion hurt me?" Giovanni asked.

"Of course not," Bruno replied. "The King of Cats has gone through a lot of trouble to bring you here."

"But why?" the boy asked, edging a bit closer to his good friend Bruno.

"Because he needs your help. The King wants you to feed the little cats that roam the upper levels. He wants you to take them fish heads every afternoon after school."

"Wow! I would love to! But what are you going to do?"

The Labyrinth

"I'm going to stay here with the King of Cats. I have grown old and tired and need a rest. So I will stay here in this beautiful garden where I have everything I need. You can come to visit me once in a while," Bruno replied.

Giovanni was delighted. He had found Bruno, and the King of Cats wanted him to feed the little cats that roamed the upper levels. He couldn't wait to get home and tell his mother and father the good news.

But Bruno warned him, "You must promise to keep your adventures into the labyrinth a secret. No one must know about the secret passageway — no one but you."

"Of course," Giovanni promised.

He said goodbye to Bruno and ran up the dark passageway until he came to the room where the Leaders lived. He heard the policeman shouting his name, and each time he said "Giovanni" his name echoed off the walls. He tapped on the stones and the door shut. Then he followed the echoes until he found the policeman.

"At last!" the policeman exclaimed. "I was afraid I would never get out of here. You're the only one who knows the way through all these dark rooms and corridors. How do we get out?"

"Follow me," Giovanni replied.

He grabbed the policeman's big hand and led him to the door that opened out onto the street. Giovanni had expected the sunshine to hurt his eyes, but the sun had already set. The only light that greeted him was the light shining from the windows of his mother's kitchen. How could there have been so much light where Bruno and the King live? Maybe the sun never sets in the Kingdom of Cats. That would be nice, he thought.

He sniffed the air. He could smell the oregano and bay leaves simmering in his mother's spaghetti sauce. "Um, um," he said, rubbing his stomach. His adventure had made him hungry. He ran across the cobblestones to his house as fast as he could because he was late for dinner.

The Magic Mystery Ball

Written & Illustrated
by Sylvia Schmit

Down in the meadow
Where the June bugs trill,
Hidden by the bluebells,
Nestled 'neath a hill,
Dwells the lovely Princess Mouse
Singing low when all is still.

Across the shining rivers,
Past a gleaming waterfall,
Through the ancient forest
Where the golden warblers call,
Speeds the noble Squire Mouse
With his Magic Mystery Ball.

Spun of love's soft fancy
From a silvery moon-mist beam,
Woven of gentle glances
Betokening fond esteem,
It brings a joy undying
To those who know to dream.

Grandfather's Piano

by Dorothy Motry Knudson

Caroline was so excited she twisted her long blond hair into knots and tapped one patent leather slipper against the other. She was going to visit her grandmother. Both the plane ride and visiting her grandmother were exciting enough, but what she was really looking forward to was seeing her grandfather's piano. It was like having a dream come true. Ever since she could remember she had listened to stories about her grandfather, who had been one of the greatest concert pianists the world had ever known.

Besides being a great musician, he had been decidedly eccentric. Caroline had been brought up on tales of Grandfather's peculiarities. The one she liked best was about his piano. He was always reluctant to play on any piano but his own, and it had traveled around the world with him, at great expense and inconvenience. Mr. Redfield, who used to be Grandfather's manager and who had arranged his concert tours, said that Grandfather used to talk to the piano as though it were a real person. Now Caroline was going to see the piano she had heard so much about, touch it — perhaps Grandmother would let her play it. She had been taking piano lessons since she was six, but although she practiced every day and tried very hard, she didn't think she would ever be able to play half as well as her grandfather.

When the plane landed the stewardess came hurrying up and said, "Come, Caroline, you are going to be the first one off the plane."

Caroline saw her grandmother before her grandmother had recognized her. "I wasn't expecting you to have grown so much since I saw you last year," she said.

It took a long time for Grandmother to drive to Ferndale, but when the car stopped in front of her house, Caroline cried, "Oh, it looks just the way Daddy described it!" It was a large house with a high peaked roof and a balcony with a wrought iron fence around it. Guarding the front steps was the huge iron frog her father had told her about.

Grandmother was hanging up their coats when the doorbell rang. "Now who could that be?" asked Grandmother. She opened the door and saw a short, fat man with a cigar in his mouth. He removed it and said, "Are you Mrs. Radtke? Mrs. Paul Radtke?"

"Yes, I am," replied Grandmother.

The man popped the cigar back into his mouth and held out his hand. "I'm Mr. Grant, Mr. Sid Grant, and I've come to make you an offer for Mr. Radtke's piano."

"But I don't want to sell the piano," said Grandmother. "Why, I spend half an hour every day polishing it. What would I do without it?"

"If you didn't have it, you wouldn't have to polish it, lady," said the man.

"But I like to polish it."

"Well," said the man, "what would you say to an offer of $10,000?"

"I don't need $10,000, and I want to keep the piano," said Grandmother. "All I have to do is close my eyes and I can see Paul seated at the piano practicing for his next concert tour. In the evenings the people of Ferndale would gather on the porch and on the steps to hear Paul play. Why, that piano has been all over the world. It's more than just a piano — why, it's part of Paul. Thank you for your offer, but I couldn't ever sell his piano."

"Listen, lady, I'll make it $15,000."

"No," replied Grandmother, "the piano isn't for sale."

"$20,000!" shouted the fat little man. "And that's my last offer."

"I'm sorry," said Grandmother, "but the piano isn't for sale at any price."

"$25,000!" said the man, almost in a whisper this time. "I'll give you until tomorrow to think about it," and he turned and walked down the steps, angrily chewing on the end of his cigar.

Caroline breathed a sigh of relief. "I'm glad you didn't sell it," she said, following her grandmother into the large front parlor. At one end of the room stood a gleaming grand piano. Here and there were numerous dents and scratches, but it was polished so well that it seemed to be enveloped in a halo. In front of it was the iron bench that Paul Radtke always used, and which had traveled with the piano from one city to another and one country to another. Hanging on the wall behind the piano was a large oil painting of the famous pianist, painted by an equally famous artist.

Caroline wanted to touch the keys, but she didn't know whether she should or not.

"Come," said Grandmother, "I have a pitcher of lemonade and a plate of oatmeal cookies in the kitchen." She led the way to the old-fashioned kitchen that smelled of freshly baked oatmeal cookies. She filled a plate with the spicy cookies, placed it on the table, and took a pitcher of lemonade out of the refrigerator. While everything else Caroline had seen so far was just the way Daddy had described it, a large, gleaming refrigerator had replaced the icebox they had used when her father was a boy.

After Caroline had completely emptied the plate of cookies and most of the lemonade had disappeared, she was hoping she could go back in the front parlor and play the piano. Before she had summoned up enough courage to ask, however, Grandmother suggested that they go out in the garden and pick some raspberries for supper. That was something else Daddy had told her about — picking raspberries and cherries. She was anxious to see the cherry tree, too. Daddy had fallen out of it and broken his arm when he was a little boy. A large, fat cat lay sleeping in the sunshine on the back porch steps.

"That's Clarence," said Grandmother, carefully stepping over him. "He's older than you are. I've had him since he was a little kitten. He's a wonderful mouser and he never bothers the birds."

Caroline thought he looked too old and lazy to bother anything, even mice. She carefully stepped over him.

The yard was filled with flowers. Every flower Caroline could think of was there. There was also a little vegetable garden, and behind that the raspberries and strawberries. It was fun to pick the soft, ripe raspberries. Some she put in her grandmother's pail and some she put in her mouth.

It wasn't until after supper and her third dish of raspberries that Caroline had an opportunity to play Grandfather's piano. She and her grandmother were sitting in the parlor looking at pictures of Daddy when he was a little boy and pictures of Grandfather taken all over the world. They had looked at the last picture, so Grandmother put the albums away in the old-fashioned bookcase. Caroline knew that Grandmother would think of something else to do if she didn't ask her quickly. She might even suggest going to bed. Caroline gripped the arms of her chair to give her courage and plunged right in. "Grandmother," she asked hurriedly, so that the words tumbled all over each other, "I've been taking piano lessons for three years. Mother thinks I play very well, and Daddy thinks I play pretty well, for a little girl. Please, may I play Grandfather's piano? I'll be very careful and just play softly. Please, Grandmother, may I?"

The Green Tiger's Caravan

Grandmother closed the door of the bookcase, locked it, and dropped the key in the blue vase on top of the bookcase. Then she turned around and said, "Of course you may play the piano, Caroline, but you will find it very hard to play. Everyone who tries it finds the keys too stiff and hard to press down, but try it if you like."

Caroline was very disappointed to hear this, but she hurried to the piano to try, anyway. She seated herself on the iron bench, spread out her skirt, and gently placed her hands on the keys. The keys went down with almost no effort. She began to play a waltz that Grandfather had composed when her daddy had been a little boy. It was familiar to music lovers the world over. Caroline had practiced it for two years, and her piano teacher thought she played it very well, for a little girl. Caroline agreed with her. Today, however, she was amazed how well and how fast she was playing it. The keys seemed to go down almost before she struck the notes. Grandfather's piano was wonderful to play! No wonder he took it everywhere with him. She finished the waltz triumphantly and turned to her grandmother, "Why, it doesn't play hard at all! It's a wonderful piano! Oh, Grandmother, don't ever sell it!"

Grandmother was looking at Caroline with astonishment. "Why, Caroline," she said, "you play very well for a child. You must have remarkably strong fingers. No one else has been able to play that piano for years. But maybe it's loosened up," she added. She poked at the piano experimentally with one finger. The keys were stiff and unyielding. "My gracious, child! You must have very strong fingers. I wonder if we are going to have another famous pianist in the family." Caroline was wondering, too. She knew she had never played so well before. She wanted to play some more, but Grandmother said, "You may play the piano tomorrow. It's getting late now, and I'm sure you are tired after your long trip."

Caroline went upstairs to the room that used to be her father's and got ready for bed. Just before she went to sleep she thought about the fat little man with the cigar who had wanted to buy Grandfather's piano. She hoped he wouldn't come back and make Grandmother change her mind.

The next morning, while her grandmother was picking peas for dinner, Caroline sat down at the piano and sighed happily. She played major and minor scales, chords and arpeggios. She tried to play several little pieces that she had learned, but she couldn't quite remember them. The truth was, she knew only one piece really well and that was the waltz she had played for Grandmother last night. She decided to play it over again. It sounded even better this morning. She was very pleased with herself, and thought, "Someday I'll be famous, too." As she sat there, pleasantly dreaming, she heard a voice say, "Well, can't you play anything else but that tinkly waltz?"

Caroline looked behind her in surprise. It certainly wasn't Grandmother's voice, and she knew her grandmother wouldn't be that rude. It sounded like a man's voice. Caroline got up and ran to look in the dining room and kitchen. There was no one there. She went back to the piano. There was no one there. As she glanced around the room, her eyes rested on Grandfather's portrait. He seemed to be looking directly at her. She shivered. But it couldn't have been Grandfather's portrait talking to her! What a silly thought! She looked up at the portrait, again. Grandfather seemed to be smiling at her. Well, if the portrait really could talk, she certainly didn't want to run away. There were a number of things she wanted to ask her grandfather: how many hours a day he had practiced and how long it took to become famous. She felt a little foolish and just a little afraid, but looking at Grandfather directly in the eye, she asked, "Did you speak to me, sir?"

"I did," said a high-pitched falsetto voice. "I said, can't you play anything else?"

Caroline jumped. It certainly couldn't be Grandfather's voice this time. It sounded like a Walt Disney character.

Grandfather's Piano

"I can't see anyone, and why are you disguising your voice? I'm going to call Grandmother."

"Wait," said the voice, now deep and rumbly again. "I wasn't disguising my voice. I was just speaking through my treble. It's like talking through your nose," and the voice ended on a high note.

Suddenly, while Caroline watched in astonishment, the keys of the piano went down all by themselves and played a brief arpeggio. Caroline pinched herself to see if she hadn't fallen asleep at the piano. "Ouch!" she said. She was awake all right, and there was no doubt about it, the piano *was* talking!

"How can a piano talk?" she asked, wonderingly.

"I'm a very famous piano. Didn't you hear that fat man offer $25,000 for me?"

"Does he know you can talk?" asked Caroline.

"Of course not! I don't talk to strangers," said the piano through his treble.

"Does Grandmother know you can talk?"

"I should say not! If she knew I could talk, she'd talk me to death! As it is, she talks to herself sometimes."

"Did Grandfather know you could talk?"

"Of course he did. We used to discuss everything from sharps to flats. Why do you think he took me with him all over the world?" he asked gruffly. "So he would have someone to talk to. He used to ask my advice about everything. Well, as I was saying, can't you play anything but that insipid waltz?"

"Insipid!" gasped Caroline. "Why, Grandfather wrote it and I think it's beautiful. I think I play it very well, too."

The piano laughed through his bass. "With me helping you."

"How could you help me?" asked Caroline, indignantly. "Why, I've practiced that waltz for two years."

The piano sighed. "I've played it 10,951 times, and I don't want to play it again, ever! I'm sick and tired of it!" he roared.

"Hush!" said Caroline, in alarm. "Grandmother will hear you."

The kitchen door slammed shut, and Grandmother came hurrying into the parlor. She glanced around the room. "Was someone here, Caroline? I thought I heard someone talking."

"Oh, no! There's no one here, Grandmother. I was just reciting," she said, glancing nervously at the piano. She clasped her hands behind her back, threw her shoulders back, and began:

'I stood on the bridge at midnight,
the clock was striking the hour —'

"Oh, yes," smiled Grandmother, "your Daddy had to memorize that when he went to school. But it's such a lovely day, wouldn't you rather come outside with me? You can pick some flowers for the parlor."

Caroline hastily snipped off some snapdragons and roses and arranged them in a bowl. Then she carried it into the parlor and placed it on a desk in a corner of the room.

"Well," said the piano, "*can* you play anything else?"

"Of course I can," said Caroline quickly, "but I forgot my music."

"Music!" said the piano, impatiently. "Why, that mahogany cabinet over there is full of music."

Timidly, Caroline looked through the music on the top shelf. It looked terribly difficult. Most of it she had never even heard of.

The Green Tiger's Caravan

"I'm afraid I don't know how to play any of these," said Caroline, in a low voice.

"Look on the bottom shelf," suggested the piano.

Caroline pulled out a book of piano solos. While she didn't know any of them as well as the waltz, she had played a few of the easier ones. She carried it over to the piano. "I can't play them very well," she said, timidly, "but I'd like to try — if you don't mind."

"All right, all right," said the piano impatiently. "Let's begin with Chopin's Minute Waltz. Your grandfather used to tell everyone he could play it in three-quarters of a minute and spend the other quarter of a minute picking his teeth."

"Could he?" asked Caroline.

"Of course not. It was just one of his jokes."

Caroline started the Minute Waltz slowly and carefully as she had been taught, but she found her fingers flying faster and faster over the keys. Faster and faster went the music. Caroline was amazed. She had never played like this before. She came to the run at the end of the waltz, a run that she knew was supposed to be played very fast, but before she could even start it, it had ended.

"I wish you wouldn't be in such a hurry," said Caroline. "I can play that run myself."

"I can't wait all day," said the piano crossly.

"All day!" objected Caroline. "Why, I've never played it *that* slowly."

"If I hadn't helped you, you'd still be struggling along with it," said the piano in a superior tone. "Can't you play even one concerto?" asked the piano hopefully.

"Concerto?"

"I can see that you can't," said the piano in a disappointed voice, deep and rumbly. "Well, it's more fun to play with an orchestra, anyway." He sighed. "Can you play Beethoven's Appassionata Sonata?" he asked, not too hopefully.

"Of course not!" said Caroline. "Even my teacher can't play that!"

"Hmph! Well, you're going to play it right now. Go over to the cabinet and get the music."

Caroline did as she was told. She opened the music and propped it up on the piano. The pages were yellow and ragged. There were pencilled notes all over the pages.

"Now," said the piano, gleefully, "let's begin!"

"But I can't," protested Caroline. "It's much too difficult."

"I certainly don't need any help from you," said the piano, rudely. "I've played it 3,000 times. I could play it in my sleep. It's one of my favorites. But I haven't played it since your grandfather died."

Caroline placed her hands on the keyboard and tried to play the opening bars of the sonata.

"Keep your hands off my keyboard," said the piano. "I'll play this by myself. Just sit there with your hands in your lap, and if anyone comes, pretend you are playing."

"All right," said Caroline, "but play softly."

The piano started out softly, but in a moment the room echoed with the lovely sonata. The music grew louder and louder.

"Hush," said Caroline, "Grandmother will hear you."

"What if she does?" chuckled the piano. "She'll think it's you. Listen to this," and he began the lovely andante movement. It was so lovely that Caroline forgot everything but the music that filled the room. The kitchen door closed quietly this time, as Grandmother crept softly across the kitchen and through the dining room and into the parlor. On her face was a look of disbelief and wonder. Then she stared in amazement. Seated at the piano was her own granddaughter! The framework of the piano hid Caroline's hands and the keyboard from view. "It couldn't be!" thought Grandmother. No one but Paul Radtke could play like that.

Grandfather's Piano

Just then Caroline caught sight of her grandmother in the doorway, tears streaming down her cheeks. "Hush," she said softly to the piano. The music came to an abrupt end. Caroline felt glued to the piano bench. She didn't know how to explain to her grandmother that the piano could play all by itself. But probably Grandmother did know now. She certainly couldn't expect her to believe it was her, Caroline, playing the sonata. Suddenly Caroline jumped up in alarm. Grandmother had slowly fallen to the floor in a faint. "Now see what you've done," she whispered fiercely to the piano. She ran over to her grandmother who lay quiet and still on the floor.

"Oh, she's as healthy as an ox. You should have her polish your legs every morning," said the piano in a high whisper. "Just throw a glass of water in her face. She'll be all right."

Caroline was on her way to the kitchen for a glass of water when the doorbell rang. With a sigh of relief, Caroline ran to open the door. There on the porch stood the little fat man with the cigar in his mouth and a tall, thin, excited elderly lady in a tweed suit and a drab black straw hat. They stared in alarm at Mrs. Radtke lying on the floor. Caroline decided they wouldn't be much help after all. She ran into the kitchen and got a glass of water. When she returned, the tall, thin lady was sitting on the floor with Grandmother's head in her lap. Caroline hesitated a moment and then emptied the contents of the glass in Grandmother's face. Like water running down hill, the water slid off Grandmother's face and made a cold, uncomfortable pool in the thin lady's lap.

Slowly Grandmother opened her eyes and sat up. She stared at Caroline. "It sounded like your grandfather playing," she said in a weak voice. She continued to stare at Caroline. The fat man stared at the thin lady's skirt, which was wet and dripping. She tried ineffectively to soak up the water with a tiny, lace hankerchief.

All at once Grandmother noticed that she had company. "Good afternoon, Miss Bradley," she said. Miss Bradley helped Grandmother over to the davenport.

"Oh, it's you," she said to the little fat man. "The piano still isn't for sale. It'll never be for sale. We have another famous musician in the family now." She patted Caroline's hand.

"Her?" said the fat man. "Don't tell me it was that little girl playing the piano."

Miss Bradley dropped her hankerchief in surprise and stared at Caroline. "Do you mean to tell me *she* was playing the piano a few minutes ago?" She pointed a skinny finger at Caroline. "I heard the music as I was passing by and came in to see who could be playing."

Caroline sat on the davenport next to her grandmother. Her cheeks were red with embarrassment. She didn't want them to think she was playing the sonata. But how could she explain? They would never believe that the piano was playing all by itself. She could hardly believe it herself. If Mr. Grant knew the piano could play all by itself, he would be even more anxious to have it. She'd never tell him that.

Mr. Grant came up closer. He had forgotten the piano for the moment. "Were you playing the piano?" he asked sharply.

"Were you?" asked the skinny lady, taking a notebook and pencil out of her purse. Miss Bradley was the society reporter for the Ferndale News, and it looked as though she was going to have a very interesting item for the evening paper.

"Of course she was," said Grandmother. "I saw her with my own eyes. That's why I fainted. It was such a shock to see such a small girl playing Beethoven's Appassionata Sonata exactly as Paul played it."

"Oh, Grandmother! I wasn't playing it! It was the piano," cried Caroline, unable to keep quiet any longer.

"No doubt her grandfather's piano has been an inspiration to her," said Grandmother.

Caroline saw that it was useless to try to explain.

The Green Tiger's Caravan

"Listen," said the fat man, talking so fast that his cigar wobbled up and down, "I'll be her business manager. We'll travel all over the country. She'll play before the crowned heads of Europe. We'll make a fortune." He clasped his fat hands together and beamed at Caroline.

"Don't you read the newspapers?" asked Miss Bradley. "There isn't a handful of crowned heads left in Europe."

"She's too young to travel all around the country," said Grandmother. "But maybe we could arrange a concert in New York or Philadelphia," she added thoughtfully.

"Fine, fine!" said Mr. Grant. "I'll arrange it at once."

"You aren't her manager until you've been hired," said Grandmother, firmly. "If Caroline needs a manager, I'll let you know. Good day!" she said, getting to her feet and opening the door. Mr. Sid Grant gave one last look at the piano and then walked slowly and regretfully out of the house.

After Miss Bradley found out Caroline's age, where she lived, what grade she was in, and all about her, she left and hurried to her office to write a story about Caroline for the Ferndale News.

"Well," said Grandmother, "I'll certainly have a surprise for my sewing circle tomorrow."

"What surprise?" asked Caroline, puzzled.

"My sewing circle meets tomorrow," explained Grandmother," and when they hear you play, they are going to be very surprised."

"Oh, I couldn't play for them," gasped Caroline. "Please don't ask me to."

"Of course you can," said Grandmother. "Why, you may be playing before thousands of people before very long. You are only a child and already you play as well as your grandfather."

As soon as her grandmother went outdoors again, Caroline went over to the piano and sat down on the bench. "Now see what you've done," she said softly. "What am I going to do?"

"Do?" chuckled the piano softly. "We're going to travel all over the world together, you and I. Never a dull moment. There'll be things to do and see and hear." He breathed a sigh of relief. "It's been pretty dull just sitting here for the past twelve years and being polished day after day. My legs ache from so much polishing. But it does keep the mice from gnawing on my legs and climbing up to build their nests inside me. They don't like the smell of the polish," he explained.

"Mice," said Caroline in surprise. "Does Grandmother have mice in her house?"

"Dozens of them," replied the piano. "Most of them live in the cellar. One has a nest in back of the bookcase. It's too heavy to move and your grandmother never sweeps behind it. Her eyes aren't as sharp as they used to be. Why, I've seen them scamper right under her nose, and she doesn't even see them!"

"But what about Clarence?" asked Caroline.

"Clarence!" snorted the piano in disgust. "He's too lazy to catch them. All he does is sleep. If it weren't for the mice, though, life would be just too dull around here — nothing but the sewing circle."

"Speaking of the sewing circle," said Caroline, sharply, "what am I going to do tomorrow?"

"Let's give them a real concert," chuckled the piano. "We'll play everything your grandfather played."

"Don't be silly," said Caroline crossly. "They will be watching my hands, and the only thing I can play is the waltz."

"Well, play it then," said the piano in a resigned voice. "If they can stand it, I can."

"But they will ask me to play the sonata. They'll all read about it in the paper tonight.

Grandfather's Piano

What'll I do?" asked Caroline desperately. "I could fall out of the cherry tree and break my arm, like Daddy," she said, thoughtfully.

"You might break your neck instead," cautioned the piano. Suddenly he chuckled in his bass and laughed in his treble.

"Hush!" said Caroline. "I don't think it's funny."

"You will," promised the piano. "Just play that silly waltz tomorrow, and if they ask you to play the sonata, just leave everything to me. Oh, boy! Are we going to have fun!"

By two o'clock the next afternoon, Caroline was dressed in her best pink ruffled dress. Two pink satin bows perched in her hair like tiny butterflies. She thought about how much she would have enjoyed getting dressed in her best dress and playing the waltz for the ladies — if only there hadn't been the misunderstanding about her playing the sonata. She scowled at the piano.

"Don't look so cross," said the piano in a whisper. "I'll take care of everything."

Before Caroline could answer, the doorbell rang, announcing the arrival of the president, the vice president, the secretary, and the treasurer of the sewing circle. Following closely, came fifteen short and fat, tall and thin members of the organization, all of whom patted Caroline on the head, shook her hand, and beamed at her as though they had found a Christmas tree in Mrs. Radtke's parlor in the middle of July.

Caroline sat in a corner by the bookcase while the secretary read the minutes of the last meeting and the president made a few announcements. Once or twice Caroline thought she heard a squeaking noise coming from behind the bookcase. She tucked her feet under her and shivered. Then she heard the president of the sewing circle saying, "Today, as you all know, we have a very special treat in store for us." Every eye was on Caroline as she went slowly to the piano, spread out her pink ruffled skirt, and began to play the waltz. When she finished she got up from the piano quickly and went and sat down in the chair by the bookcase.

The ladies clapped politely, but they were plainly disappointed.

"That was very pretty, dear, but won't you play the Beethoven sonata for us? Miss Bradley said you played it exactly the way your grandfather played it."

Caroline began nervously twisting her long blonde hair into knots.

"Play the sonata for them, Caroline," said her grandmother, smiling proudly.

Before Grandmother had finished speaking, a small army of little brown mice raced from behind the bookcase and scampered in all directions. Scampering in all directions went the short and fat, tall and thin ladies. Some ran out the front door, some ran out the back door — but they all ran out of the house. The kitchen door opened and then slammed shut again and Caroline heard her grandmother say, "There! I'll put Clarence inside. He'll quickly frighten them all away. I wonder where they all came from."

Clarence strolled leisurely into the parlor, lay down in front of the bookcase, and went to sleep. A little brown mouse, hurrying back to his home behind the bookcase, ran by him so close their whiskers touched.

"Now that I got rid of the ladies for you, let's play the sonata. Let's play two sonatas, four nocturnes, and a few rhapsodies," said the piano, excitedly.

"No," said Caroline firmly, "not until I really can play them. Of course, I wouldn't mind if you helped me a little — if no one notices. But I'm going to practice and practice and practice until I can play all of Grandfather's music. Then, when I really can play almost as well as Grandfather, we'll travel all over the world together — just as you and Grandfather did."

The piano sighed. "I'll be polished away to a mere shadow by then."

"I'll tell Grandmother so much polishing isn't good for you," said Caroline. "Anyway," she smiled, "I think Grandmother will be too busy trying to catch all those mice to bother polishing you every day. If I told her it was your idea to have the mice chase the ladies out of the house, she'd probably sell you to Mr. Grant."

"Couldn't we just play one little sonata?" pleaded the piano.

"No," said Caroline, reluctantly. "Not until I can play it *almost* by myself. You see," she explained, "if anyone found out you can play all by yourself, you'd be much more famous than you are now. Why, people would come from all over to see you. They'd fill the house, the garden, even the town of Ferndale. People would whack chunks out of you and pull your keys off to take home for souvenirs."

"Stop!" cried the piano in a voice of anguish. "I'll wait until you can play better. I don't want to be cut up and pulled to pieces. I won't even mind your grandmother polishing my legs. But for goodness sake, don't forget to practice every day. Your grandfather practiced six hours a day."

"I'll practice and practice and practice," promised Caroline, "until I'm almost as good as Grandfather."

"Ho hum!" said the piano. "I think I'll take a nice long nap while you're practicing and practicing," he added, sleepily. "I'm going to be dreaming about the concert tour you and I are going to make some day. New York, Philadelphia, Chicago, London, Paris..." He sighed through his bass, yawned through his treble, and went sound to sleep.

THE CARPENTER PUZZLED

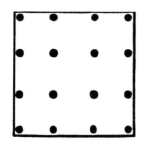

A ship having sprung a leak at sea, and being in great danger, the carpenter could find nothing to mend it with, except a piece of wood, of which the annexed is a correct representation; supposing the black dots in it to represent holes in the wood, thus apparently preventing him from cutting out of it the sized piece he wanted, which was exactly one quarter of the board. Required, the way in which he must cut this piece of wood, to obtain out of it a piece exactly one-fourth its own size having no holes in it.

THE GRASPING LANDLORD

Suppose a certain landlord had eight apple trees around his mansion, around these eight houses of his tenants, around these ten pear trees,—he wants to have the whole of the pear trees to himself, and allot to each of his tenants one of his apple trees in their place. How must he construct a fence or hedge to accomplish it?

Answers, p. 88

The Garden

by Susan Harvey

There was a man living in a garden, and it was almost time for him to leave.

Sooner or later, everyone who lived in the garden had to leave, and every creature was allowed to choose something to take along.

On his last day, the man got up early and went about his chores. As he worked he thought what he would choose, for he dearly loved the garden and everything in it.

He loved the flowers. He loved the insects. He loved the tools with which he worked. He loved the cat. He even loved the wall and the path and the pond.

In the morning the flowers spoke to him. "Choose us," they said. "You know how much you love to look at us and breathe our fragrance. Choose us, and then when you leave the garden you will still keep something beautiful."

"Yes," said the man. "You have given me much pleasure. But you couldn't live outside the garden. You belong here." And he thanked the flowers and said goodbye to them.

When the sun was high in the sky the insects spoke to him. "Choose us," they said. "You know how well we have taken care of you. We are very dependable. Choose us and when you leave the garden you will still have something to depend on."

"It's true," said the man. "You have been a great help to me." For the bees had made honey for him, and the silkworms had spun silk for him, and the ants had helped with moving things about. "But the garden needs you more than I will. Stay here and carry on." And he thanked the insects and said goodbye to them.

In the afternoon, as he was tidying up after his chores were done, his tools spoke to him. "Choose us," they said. "After all, you are a gardener, and gardeners need their tools. Choose us, and when you leave the garden you will still be able to earn your living."

"All that is so," said the man. "But where I am going there may not be any gardens." And he thanked his tools, and cleaned them, and carefully put them away.

Towards evening the cat wandered across the grass to where the man was sitting. Neither spoke for awhile. But finally the cat said, "Ahem!"

The man smiled.

"I suppose," said the cat, "that you've chosen what you're going to take with you."

"No, I haven't," said the man.

"How about me, then?" said the cat. "We've been friends for a long time. You might get very lonely out there, you know. Choose me, and when you leave the garden you will still have a friend."

"I will miss you most of all," said the man as he stroked the cat's beautiful neck. "And I will always remember you. But I won't choose you."

And at this the cat stalked away and began to sulk.

"I am trying to remember," went on the man, "something that I saw once that I knew would be the best thing to choose. Perhaps I told you about it — do you remember?"

The cat pretended not to hear. He washed his face and he checked between his toes. He straightened his whiskers. At last he said, "Oh, all right," and he started off down the path that led to the pond. "Come on," he said,

They came to the pond just as the sun was setting. "Sit down here and wait," the cat said to the man. "If you sit quietly and watch carefully you'll remember." And he turned to go.

"Thank you," said the man. "Goodbye."

"You're welcome," said the cat. "Goodbye."

So the man sat and watched as the sun crept lower down the sky, and he felt a little sad, and a little bit afraid, but he waited and watched, because he trusted the cat, who was his friend.

And then all of a sudden the last sunbeams came leaping onto the pond, and the pond began to laugh to feel them dancing there, and everything turned golden and singing and the man remembered what to choose.

The man sat watching and the golden light fell upon him, too, as his last day in the garden ended.

And when he awoke, he was somewhere else.

WORD SQUARES

Word squares must read the same down and across. The words are described and you must guess them from their descriptions.

```
H O M E
O V E N
M E N D
E N D S
```

1.

1. Flies with the wind.
2. Smooths the clothes.
3. Hops and catches flies.
4. The last of things.

2.

1. A gift of winter.
2. Given to you when you were a baby: lasts your lifetime.
3. A sign.
4. Means did go.

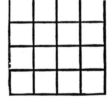

3.

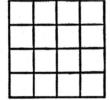

1. Found in sea water.
2. Slightly open
3. Not on time.
4. The tallest plant.

Answers, p. 88

60

Pete's Magical Cement Mixer

by Virginia B. Deans
illustrated by Susan Tereba

For six months, Pete sat in his little shack in the woods waiting for someone to hire him and his cement mixer for a job. Pete's cement mixer was small and old-fashioned and didn't make very good concrete anymore, but Pete still hoped for one more big job before he retired for good.

One day, Pete got a letter. It was from Mayor O'Riley, from the town of Tipsum. Mayor O'Riley wanted to hire Pete to fill the potholes in their town streets.

He couldn't pay very much, he explained in his letter, because the town was very poor. Pete was delighted and accepted immediately.

It was still dark when Pete filled his mixer with sand, gravel, and cement and motored over to the town of Tipsum. No one was up yet when he started to work. He filled all the potholes in all the streets of Tipsum. When he was done, he looked back at his work. He couldn't believe his eyes. The potholes were a beautiful shade of violet! They reminded him of violets growing deep in a wooded glen.

"How in the world did that happen?" he wondered out loud. What would the townspeople think when they saw violet circles all over their streets?

Not even waiting to be paid, Pete drove out of town as fast as he could. When he arrived home, he washed out the cement mixer and got rid of the violet concrete. He couldn't imagine what he had done wrong.

For a week, Pete worried and wondered if the mayor would make him dig up the potholes again. One morning, he awoke to a hammering on the door. It was the mayor in person. "We love what you did to our streets!" he exclaimed, throwing his arms around Pete. "At first, the townspeople were upset, but soon word spread far and wide about Tipsum's violet polka-dots! Already, the tourist trade has begun to make our citizens prosperous." He handed Pete twice the amount of money he had promised to pay.

Pete was so surprised he couldn't think of a thing to say.

The mayor continued. "The potholes were such a success that the council voted more funds for a violet driveway leading to the Town Hall." He winked at Pete. "If violet potholes bring in a hundred tourists, the addition of a violet driveway should bring in twice as many, don't you think?"

Pete agreed and promised to pave their driveway the next day.

Bright and early the next morning, Pete filled his mixer with sand, gravel, and cement and motored over to the town of Tipsum. When he reached the Town Hall, he tipped up the mixer and poured concrete from the road to the front doorstep.

When he was through, he looked back at his work. He blinked. He blinked again. It wasn't violet at all, but a beautiful golden yellow! It reminded him of a misty meadow of golden buttercups.

The townspeople crowded around the golden driveway. At first, they were disappointed because it wasn't violet. Then they realized that violet polka-dots and a golden driveway were better than having everything violet. They clapped Pete on the back and cheered. The beaming mayor paid Pete and sent him on his way.

On the road home, Pete scratched his head. Why was his cement a different color every time he made it? It was always gray before. What was he doing different? He thought and thought, but he couldn't figure out the answer.

Now that Pete had been paid for both jobs, he was ready to retire. He puttered happily around his yard and tended his vegetable garden.

It was time to retire his cement mixer too. Pete built a carport next to his shack and parked it there. "We might as well be comfortable in our old age," he said, patting his machine.

Deep inside the mixer, he heard a rumble that sounded very much like a burp. Shaking his head, he turned and pulled a couple of turnips from his garden for his dinner that night.

One day, in the early fall, Mayor O'Riley came again to Pete's shack. Pete hardly recognized him because he had grown so fat. He was puffing on a big cigar and looked very prosperous.

"I have another job for you," he said. "Tipsum has become the most famous town around and also the richest. The violet polka-dots and the golden driveway to the Town Hall have been viewed by tourists the world over!"

Pete was surprised his concrete had caused such a stir, but he was happy to hear it.

"The council has voted funds for a road to be built completely around the town, and we want you to pave it in one of your marvelous colors."

"Around the town?" Pete asked, scratching his head. "That would be a circle going no place."

"Where it goes doesn't matter," the mayor chuckled. "The only thing we care about is its color."

That was a big job, and Pete liked his retirement. He didn't want to do it and said so. When the mayor told him how much the town was counting on him, Pete finally agreed to do it.

That night, he went to bed a worried man. He had no control over the color of his concrete. In fact he hadn't made a batch since the golden driveway. What if he turned out the _____ _____ he used to make? If only it was colorful this one last time, he would _____ and tossing fitfully, he finally fell asleep.

_____ _____ his cement mixer shifted its gears and moseyed off into the woods. Following along a well-worn path, he came to a glen filled with violets. After a moment's hesitation, he continued on through a misty meadow of golden buttercups. When he came to a broad field of swaying bluebells, he stopped and sniffed. He nipped one neatly off the stem. "Delicious!" he sighed, and he ate them all up.

The Taxi with the Two-Way Stretch

by Addie Adam
illustrated by Jeff Carnehl

On the day of the big baseball game between Plattsville and Blottsville, the bus and taxi drivers decided to have a strike. With the game held fifteen miles away, in Blottsville, the people of Plattsville who did not own cars stood around in unhappy groups wondering how to get to the game.

Now, it happened that Gus, the bald-headed driver, owned his own cab and did not join the strikers.

"Come on, sports fans," he called to the sad-faced group. "I'm going to the game and I will take you."

The people looked doubtfully at Gus's cab. It was dented and battered and wrinkled and looked as if it could not make it to the ice cream parlor on the next block, much less to Blottsville, fifteen miles away. But they did not want to hurt Gus's feelings.

63

The Green Tiger's Caravan

"That's nice of you, Gus, but you can't take one hundred and fifteen people in your little cab," one man said.

"Trust me," Gus smiled. "Get in. The ride is free."

So a teacher and her pupils climbed in and the taxi was full.

"Take a deep breath and push on the cab," Gus said. "My taxi stretches two ways."

So the teacher and her pupils pushed on the sides of the cab. The taxi squeaked, and, suddenly, it was almost as wide as the road.

"Room for more," Gus called.

The farmer and his family climbed in, and the taxi was full.

"Take a deep breath and push," Gus said.

When they pushed at the rear the taxi groaned, and, suddenly, it was as long as a truck.

"Room for more," Gus called.

A scout master and his boy scout troop climbed in and the taxi was full.

"Take a deep breath and push," Gus said.

When they did, the taxi wheezed, and, suddenly, it was as long as a bus.

"Room for more," Gus called.

The men's Song Club of Plattsville climbed in, and the taxi was full.

"Take a deep breath and push," Gus said.

When they did, the taxi squeaked and wheezed and groaned, and, suddenly, it was as long as a train.

"Room for more," Gus called.

The Ladies' Aid Society climbed on, followed by the last two persons: a pin salesman and a man with a limp.

"All aboard?" Gus called. "Here we go!"

Through the town of Plattsville they drove. They had just reached the edge of town when they heard a police siren. Gus pulled over to the curb and stopped. He stuck his head out of the window. "Hi, Officer Clancy. Nice morning, isn't it?"

"Gus, do you know you went through two red lights at the corner of Maple and Oak Streets?"

Gus scratched his bald head. "How could I go through two red lights at the same corner?"

"Gus, how long is your taxi?" the officer said.

"Oh, about a quarter of a mile, I guess." Gus's eyes widened. "By thunder, you're right. My taxi is so long, I couldn't possibly get through the green light before it changed."

"Right." Clancy nodded. "You and the teacher and her pupils went through on the green light, but the farmer and his family and the scout troop crashed the red light. The Song Club went through on the green light, but the Ladies' Aid Society and the other two gentlemen crashed the red light. I'll have to give tickets to the ones who crashed the red lights."

"Stop," Gus roared. "It was my fault. I took them through, so I must pay." He took a drawstring purse from his pocket and looked inside. "Clancy, I have only enough money to get into the game."

"Just a minute," the teacher said, taking a slate and piece of chalk from her satchel. She wrote down a few numbers. "Officer, would it be all right if we each paid ten cents?"

Clancy counted the ears of everyone in the taxi and divided by two, then said, "That would just about do it."

So everybody in the taxi paid Clancy ten cents and went on their way. They had gone about a mile into the country when the taxi sputtered and stopped.

"Oh, dear, oh dear," Gus said.

"If we're out of gas," a boy scout said, "we just passed a gas station."

The Taxi With the Two-Way Stretch

"My taxi doesn't take gas," Gus explained. "It uses milk. Gas gives it heartburn."

"There is a whole field of cows," the farmer said. "I'll ask the owner if I can milk some."

The owner gave his permission, and soon the farmer was pouring twenty gallons of milk into the taxi's tank.

Each passenger paid the owner of the cows five cents, thanked him, and was soon on his way toward Blottsville on a very bumpy road.

They were ten miles from the ballpark when the taxi coughed and stopped.

Gus got out. "I think I know what's wrong." He peered into the tank. "Just as I thought," he said, "I forgot that my taxi uses only skim milk. This rough road has churned the milk. The tank is full of butter."

"Oh, dear, what will we do, now?" the ladies of the Aid Society said.

"I'm afraid you'll have to walk the rest of the way," Gus said. "I'm very sorry."

"But we can't just leave the taxi here," said the man with a limp.

"I'll stay with it and wait for a tow truck," Gus said.

"And miss the game?" the Song Club men said. "No, siree! We all go, or we all stay!"

"We can push the taxi," the scout leader suggested.

And so they pushed the taxi through farmland where a farmer's wife ran out and served them milk and cookies. They pushed it through a village where townspeople cheered them and gave them crisp carrots and lemonade.

Then, at last, Gus, who was pushing at the front, saw the ballpark gates.

"We're here!" he called back to the teacher, who passed the word back to her pupils, who passed the word back to the farmer and his family, until the word finally reached the rear where the pin salesman and the man with a limp were pushing.

"We're here!" said the men of the Song Club, who followed with a happy song.

The man with a limp looked very happy. "Somewhere on the road I lost my limp," he shouted. And the Song Club sang a song for him.

The pin salesman was quiet for a moment, then he said to the man without a limp, "I just thought of something: Gus and the others are at the gate, but we still have a quarter of a mile to walk. Oh, dear, and it's so hot!" He wiped his forehead with a red bandana.

"Oh, my, I didn't think of that." The man without a limp sat down on the bumper and wiped his face with a blue bandana.

The pin salesman sat beside him, and, as he did, some of his sample pins he carried in his pocket pricked the rear of the stretched-out taxi.

Whoosh! The air suddenly leaked out of the taxi, and the two men sitting on the bumper went sailing through the air.

The next thing they knew, they were at the gate of the ballpark, and Gus's taxi was back to its normal size.

"Thought you boys would never get here," Gus grinned. "Come on, sports fans! Let's go see the game!"

And all his one hundred and fifteen friends trooped after him through the gates, talking about how nice Gus was to give them a free ride to the ball game.

ANIMAL PUZZLE SUMS

THE ANSWER TO EACH PUZZLE ON THIS PAGE IS THE NAME OF AN ANIMAL

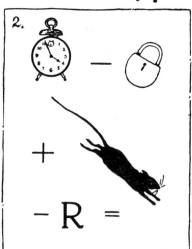

Answers, p. 88

66

This Is Not Mr. Mark Twain's
"The Celebrated Jumping Frog of Calaveras County"

by Nathan Zimelman
illustrated by Pamela Martin

It wasn't at all the way Mr. Mark Twain told it. But Mr. Mark Twain was an author, and you can't expect any better of an author. They're an almighty bunch of liars, except they call it fiction. This is the way it really happened, and I ought to know, because I was the one it happened to.

It began with Blooop who was the smartest frog in our pond. Now, being that smart and not backwards at showing it, you would expect that all the young frogs would gather about his lily pad for the learning that was there. Nothing of the sort. Except for one young and handsome frog, myself, there was no one to be seen on Blooop's lily pad but himself, talking away.

"Tad," he used to say to me, sitting at his feet, "there's more to life than perching on a lily pad waiting for a fly to come within range of your tongue. There's the wide world." And Blooop would jump into the pond.

As the water would form ever widening circles, his head would pop up in their center and he would say, "There's the wide world waiting for those willing to jump in."

Ma, who never liked Blooop, said, "A frog's place is on his lily pad and in his pond."

But I was young, not much more than a tadpole and not given to listening to Ma. After all, she never had stories to tell like Blooop did.

There's one I still remember. It had to do with a witch and a handsome frog prince magicked into an ugly man. And it all came right with a lovely lady frog waiting at the end of the story. No one's going to listen to his Ma, when there's the likes of that to be heard.

The other young frogs frolicked away the summer. They chased the glitter of dragonfly wings. They played leapfrog. They dove at the yellow sun floating on the cool green of the pond's water.

I spent the summer growing into too big a frog for such a small pond. I knew I was just going to have to leave and see that wide world Blooop was always talking about. Of course, now that I'm older, I know that Blooop was all talk and no do. There he was, pretty near the oldest frog in the pond and still there.

Like as not as I grew up, I'd have become just like Blooop, waiting for some frog, too young to know better, to come listen to me talk. Or, as was Ma's hope, I would have settled down and become a good solid frog like my Pa. The reason that neither happened is because of Jim Smiley.

Doubtless you know of Jim Smiley because of Mr. Mark Twain. If you can read, you know of Jim Smiley. Frogs can't read, words that is, so I had to meet him in person.

The first time I met him, I was sitting on the pond's mossy bank, meditating. Frogs shouldn't meditate. They should be ever watchful.

This particular day I'm telling you about, a shadow came walking along across the pond and the mossy banks about it. There was one giant splash as every frog went off its lily pad into the pond. And there I sat on the mossy bank, meditating away.

Jumping Frog

Well, I wasn't there for very long. Something clamped tightly around me, and I started to go up and up into the air. I tried to jump then. Then was just a little bit too late.

"Them's good jumping legs. He'll do! He'll more than do!"

I looked, and saw I was looking into the face of the ugliest creature I had ever seen. Toads are not as handsome as frogs, but they are passable. Birds are birds except when they are owls. But this, this had to be a man. Nothing else could be so ugly. So long a nose. And every which way hair.

I struggled with all my might. Right then I did not wish to have the wide world. I just wished to keep the world of my pond. What I got was the deep dark of a tin box and a firm fitted lid that banged my head whenever I leaped for freedom.

After some dozen bumpings, I banged enough sense into my head to stretch out to wait and see. There's nothing as beautiful as the light of the sun, when you think you are never going to see it again. All I wanted to do when I was let out of the box was to sit there and bask — which is just what I was doing when this Jim Smiley gives me what Mr. Mark Twain called a little punch in the behind.

Well, it might have been little if you were Mr. Mark Twain's size and as well developed back there as a writer gets with all the sitting he does. Being frog size I didn't find it so little. I jumped as I had never jumped before. And this Jim Smiley threw his hat down on the ground and did a dance around it.

"Oh, he's a jumper, he is, he is! Oh, he's a jumper, he is!" he kept yelling as though it was something wonderful.

Jumping is as natural with a frog as foolishness with a human being.

After that this Jim Smiley continued with my education, as Mr. Mark Twain called it. When he had done with it, and I could jump farther than any frog had a right to, we went traveling again.

It wasn't quite as bad as the first time. Jim Smiley had an old Indian fellow make me a traveling cage of willow switches, and I could at least see where I was going. It was the wide world, and it was spectacular. Mountains rising until the sky had to move aside. Trees that had forgotten to stop growing. Water rushing and falling and tearing away, mad as all get out. I would have traded it all in for one worn out lily pad in my old pond.

At last we came out to where there were a lot more human creatures that looked like Jim Smiley, only more so. It was a place called a mining camp, where human beings lived. It didn't hold a candle to a lily pad on a pond. There were big boxes everywhere with red shirted, big hatted, pantalooned and booted, bulge eyed, long nosed, bearded men rushing in and out.

I'll say this for Jim Smiley, he wasn't a rusher.

Real easy he sat himself down on a step and placed my cage between his feet, waiting. Soon enough another human creature stopped in front of him.

"What you got there?" He toed my cage.

"Frog." Jim Smiley looked everywhere but at me.

"What good is he?" the other human stuck a finger between the willow bars and wiggled at me.

"Dan'l Webster is the greatest jumper in the whole state of California." Jim Smiley smiled like he was foolish. Which he was.

"That his name?" asked the other, more foolish than Jim Smiley.

"For a frog he's as great in his line as the Senator from Massachusetts is in his. And they both can out-leap man or frog."

Jim Smiley swung the door of my cage open and set me down on the ground. "Bet you."

The Green Tiger's Caravan

"Bet," said the other human, and out of his red shirt he pulls a frog.

"Bet," said the crowd of human creatures that gathered round, watching.

Jim Smiley drew a line in the dust of the street. "Set yours next to mine," he says.

Friendly-like I tried to talk to the other frog, but big in his self importance, he would have none of it. Some frogs are a lot like human creatures.

"On the count of three." Jim Smiley held up a finger and counted.

"One." The other frog squatted, ready.

"Two." I wasn't real interested in what was going on.

"Three." Howbesoever, when Jim Smiley punched my behind, I couldn't help it. I out-leaped the other frog by a good two feet.

Jim Smiley jumped almost as far straight up, which as any frog can tell you will get you nowhere.

Anyway, not being a frog, Jim Smiley jumped straight up. Then he went around the crowd of humans, his hands held out, and they filled his cupped hands full of yellow pebbles and yellow dust which they poured from long brown sacks. Jim Smiley jumped straight up again, clicking his heels all the way down.

Jim Smiley was right happy, but why that was, I couldn't figure for the life of me. The floor of our pond was covered with yellow pebbles, and as a young frog will do, I had taken my taste. They had no worth to them.

Worth or not, Jim Smiley was eager for the yellow foolishness. He rode from mining camp to mining camp, my cage dangling from his saddle. Once arrived, down he'd sit and wait. And, sure enough, up would walk another human with a frog. The both of us would be made to toe the line. One, two, three and punch. I would fly through the air. And Jim Smiley would walk through the crowd smiling and collecting the yellow foolishness.

I don't know how long this went on. After a while everything had a sameness to it, and when one day is just like another, they just don't add up. Still and all, I guess some time must have passed, because the sack of yellow foolishness kept growing bigger and bigger.

And then we came to Angel's Camp.

How Jim Smiley could tell one place from another I do not know. They all looked pretty much alike to me. But this day that I'm about to tell you of, Jim Smiley stopped his horse in front of a board nailed to a tree and looked at some lines squiggling across the wood.

"Dan'l," he lifted my cage up to his bulging eyes, a sight I could have done without, "Dan'l, here's Angel's Camp, waiting to be took."

He gives me a punch where I'd rather he wouldn't. I jumped. Bang went my head.

"Oh, isn't he pretty!" Jim Smiley shouts to a crow watching on a limb. And into Angel's Camp we rode.

I began as it always began. Jim Smiley sat himself down real easy and placed my cage between his feet and waited. Soon enough another human stopped in front of him.

"What you got there?" He toed my cage.

Well, you know the way it goes. There isn't much difference in humans. Except this one was some unlike the others, because when Jim Smiley offered to bet, the stranger didn't reach down into his red shirt and pull out a frog. Instead he held his hands spread out and empty.

"Can't," he said. "Got no frog."

That didn't stop Jim Smiley.

"I'll get you a frog," he says.

"I'll take him." The other human reaches for my cage.

"I'd let you," Jim Smiley pulled the cage back, "if Dan'l and I didn't have a special liking for

Jumping Frog

each other."

The way it worked out, the frogless human was to hold my cage while Jim Smiley would go off and catch a frog to toe the line with me.

The way Mr. Mark Twain tells it, no sooner was Jim Smiley gone than the stranger took a teaspoon and, opening my mouth, started spooning in a full weight of quailshot. I'm not saying he wouldn't have done it, if he'd have thought of it. Howbesoever, it was Mr. Mark Twain thought of it, and right then he was standing off in the crowd squiggling pencil across paper.

So there we all stood being honest, except Mr. Mark Twain, and down the street comes Jim Smiley, dripping smiles and pond water.

"I got you a big one." Jim Smiley offers two handfuls of frog to the other human.

"Blooop! Blooop!" the frog in Jim Smiley's hand croaked.

"Blooop!" I peered between the bars of my cage. "Blooop, what are you doing here?"

And foolish as a human, old wise Blooop sat there smiling and says, "At last I've come to see the wide world."

I tell you, I didn't need any buckshot to weigh me down. My heart grew so heavy it fell right down to my bottom.

"One." Jim Smiley held up a finger.

"Two." Blooop set himself.

"Three." Jim Smiley punched.

Blooop jumped passing fair for a frog his age. I didn't move.

"THREE!" Jim Smiley came near punching clear through me.

I didn't move. I was anchored down with a heavy heart.

"Stranger," Jim Smiley turned from me, "what do you want for that frog there?"

"Come, Dan'l Webster." I felt myself rising, not clamped hard, firm yet gentle. Then down I went, into the dark. It was not the deep cold dark of a tin box, but a warm sort of rustling red shirt kind of dark.

By squinting just right I could see through a buttonhole. What I saw was the one street of Angel's Camp coming and going by. Then I saw a waving of flowers, and a reaching of trees, and what I thought was a mossy bank and green sunlight over green water, which couldn't be, because I wanted it so much to be. And then I was out of the shirt and sitting on the hands of no one less than Mr. Mark Twain.

What I was looking at was my pond. There was Ma and Pa and all the young frogs grown somewhat older. And there was a lily pad unoccupied, waiting for me.

"Daniel," Mr. Mark Twain bent and deposited me on the mossy bank, "Jim Smiley seems to have indicated he's had enough of you. And you seem to have indicated you've had enough of him. So, on behalf of the human race, accept my apology and be off with you."

He gave me a punch, and that was one punch I didn't mind, because it started a jump that landed me spang onto that lily pad in the middle of the pond.

So that is the way it all really happened, which is not the way Mr. Mark Twain told it, him being an author and given to lying, or, as he called it, fiction. But he had a good heart, and if you've got a good heart, nothing else really matters.

And that's not fiction.

Robert the Robot

by Maureen H. Barnes

One day Buddy Reed took his life savings, which was all of five dollars, and went to the store. He had just two more days to find a gift for his best friend Freddie's ninth birthday. On reaching the store, Buddy went to the second floor, where all the toys were kept. Buddy had no idea what to get Freddie, so he had to look at everything. It seemed that all the toys which he knew Freddie would like cost more than five dollars.

Finally, after half an hour of looking, Buddy came to a table full of toys with prices he could afford. After picking up a couple of toys and looking at them, Buddy knew why they were so cheap. Most of the toys had parts missing. Buddy was just about to leave the table, when something shiny caught his eye. He reached down into the pile of toys to see what it was and pulled out a silver robot. Buddy checked the robot and could find nothing wrong with it. Next he put the robot on the floor and turned it on. The robot started walking round and round in circles. Buddy couldn't believe his luck. He'd found the perfect gift for Freddie, and it only cost two dollars. With the money left over, Buddy bought a card and wrapping paper.

Buddy paid for the robot and ran home to show his mother. Mrs. Reed took one look at the robot and started laughing.

"Buddy, that's the funniest robot I've ever seen. Look at his eyes! They're two different colors: one is red, and the other is blue; and his head is almost as big as his body."

"I don't think he's funny-looking, just different. I know Freddie will just love him."

Just then Buddy's twelve-year-old sister Peggy came in. She also took one look at the robot and burst out laughing.

"Where did you find such a funny-looking robot, Buddy?"

"I bought him in a toy store. And he's not funny!"

"What are you going to do with him?" asked Peggy.

"I bought him as a birthday present for Freddie."

"You're kidding! I'd be too embarrassed to give anybody something like that."

"It's not a *that*; it's a robot, and Freddie will be crazy about him."

Peggy just shook her head as Buddy picked up his robot and went upstairs to wrap the gift for Freddie. Once in his bedroom, Buddy put the robot on his desk and began spreading the wrapping paper on his bed. After this was done, he went to the desk to get the robot. He lifted the robot up and noticed that it was wet around the eyes.

"I wonder what happened?" Buddy said aloud to the empty room. Taking his handkerchief, he dried the robot off and started to wrap him.

After wrapping the robot, Buddy put him back on the desk, and went downstairs for lunch. After lunch, Buddy took the birthday card, and went upstairs to put it with the wrapped robot. He went over to the desk but couldn't find the robot. The wrapping paper was torn up in the middle of the desk, but there was no robot. Buddy ran out of the room and headed straight for Peggy's room. There he found Peggy lying on her bed reading a book.

"Did you unwrap my robot and take him?" yelled Buddy.

"Are you kidding? Who'd want that funny-looking thing?"

"Peggy! Buddy! What's all this noise?" asked Mrs. Reed as she entered the room.

"Buddy came in here and said I took his dumb old robot."

"Well, did you?" demanded Buddy.

"No, of course I didn't take it."

"Buddy, go back to your room and look some more. You probably just put it some place and forgot where," said Mrs. Reed.

Buddy went back to his room and started looking, even though he knew he'd left the robot, wrapped, on his desk. First he looked under the desk. No robot. Next, he looked all around the room and under the bed. Still no robot. Where could he be? Buddy was just about to give up when he thought to look in his closet. He opened the door, and there, in the corner of the closet, stood the robot. Buddy picked him up and noticed that, again, his eyes were wet. He got a handkerchief, dried him off, and put him on the toy shelf next to his favorite toy, the rocket. He'd gotten it for Christmas and liked it better than any of his other toys.

That night, Buddy was sound asleep when something woke him up. He sat up in bed and listened, but heard nothing. Buddy lay back down and was almost asleep again, when a noise that sounded like crying made him sit up and turn on the light.

The noise was coming from the shelf of toys in the corner. Buddy got out of bed and went over to have a look. There, right beside his prize rocket, stood the silver robot crying. Buddy didn't believe what he was seeing. He pinched himself to make sure he wasn't dreaming.

"Ouch," he said aloud. The pinch hurt, so he must be awake.

"What's the matter, robot?" Why are you crying?"

"I'm so funny-looking, nobody likes me. Everyone is always laughing at me."

"I like you," said Buddy, "and I don't think you're funny-looking."

"If you like me, then why do you keep wrapping me up to give me away?"

"I have to. You're a birthday present."

"Please don't give me away. Let me stay with you. I can be lots of fun."

"I can't keep you, because I spent all my money and have nothing else to give Freddie. Don't worry, Freddie will like you as much as I do. Now stop crying so I can get some sleep."

"I'll stop crying, but I still think I'd be happier if you kept me."

Buddy shut off the light and went back to sleep.

The next morning Buddy woke up and went right to his toy shelf. The robot just stood there, not moving. Did he dream everything last night? He must have, because this morning the robot looked like all his other toys.

Buddy quickly got dressed and rewrapped the robot. He had just finished wrapping the robot and was putting him back on the toy shelf when his mother came in to tell him Freddie was waiting down stairs. Buddy raced downstairs to tell Freddie about the wonderful present he'd gotten him.

"You'll just love your present, Freddie. I was so lucky to find it."

"Tell me what it is, now. I can't wait till my birthday to find out."

"No, I won't tell you what it is, but since it's wrapped, I can show it to you."

Buddy and Freddie ran upstairs to see the wrapped present. When they were in the room, Freddie went all around looking for the present. Buddy quickly looked at the toy shelf and saw the robot had unwrapped himself again. He ran over and stood in front, so Freddie couldn't see it, but wasn't fast enough. Freddie had already seen the robot.

"Where'd you get that ugly-looking robot?" Freddie asked.

"He's not ugly, just different."

"He's different, all right. If it were mine, I'd throw it in the garbage. Now where's my present? I sure hope it's something nice like that rocket," said Freddie, pointing to Buddy's most prized possession.

"I'll show it to you later, but right now I have to clean up my room, so you'd better go home."

When Freddie left the room, Buddy turned around and saw that the robot was crying again.

"I told you he wouldn't like me."

"I don't understand it," said Buddy. "I think you're a wonderful toy."

"Well, you're the only one. No one else would buy me, so I was put on that table with all the broken toys. Now if you give me to Freddie, I'll be thrown away."

"Don't worry, robot. I won't give you to Freddie now."

"Please stop calling me robot; my name is Robert."

"OK, Robert. I'll stop calling you robot."

"What will you give Freddie for his birthday?" said Robert.

"I have no idea, but I'll think of something. I have to if I want to keep you."

That night, Buddy couldn't sleep. The next day was Freddie's birthday and Buddy still had nothing to give him.

During the night, an idea came to Buddy. He got up, went over to his toy shelf, and wrapped something.

The next day, Buddy went to Freddie's birthday party with his gift. Freddie opened the gift and couldn't believe his eyes. There, in his hands, was Buddy's favorite toy, the rocket.

From that day on, Robert the robot never cried again. He was now Buddy's most prized possession and stood in the place of honor on the toy shelf.

Every now and then, if you pass Buddy's room, you can hear voices and laughter when only Buddy is there.

Behold here the sight of a slippery snake.
Who rides on a bicycle of his own make.
A friendly young Spider brought over his kit,
And volunteered kindly to help him a bit,
And now any day, unless fate prove unkind,
You may see him spin by, with his friend on behind.

The Miniature Display

by Bunny Schulle
illustrated by Debbie Drechsler

Jana's daddy called her a "minutiae expert." That meant she was caught up in the world of teeny, tiny things — things that other people usually overlooked. For instance, you could always count on Jana to find a lost bead, a dropped pin in the shag rug, or a ladybug hiding behind a leaf. She might miss seeing an elephant crossing the road, but she'd spot an inchworm on that same road with no problem.

There was nothing wrong with her eyes; she merely focused upon the miniscule. She also loved collecting tiny things, and soon had every table-top in her room completely covered with her miniatures.

One day, her mother finally tired of trying to dust Jana's dresser, night table, and desk because she had to move and rearrange so many little possessions. She was always afraid of dropping something precious and then vacuuming it up. So, she took Jana to the nearest convenience store, and, for a small amount of money, they bought an empty soft drink carrier. It was made of wood and had 24 compartments to hold the bottles: four rows across and six rows down. Since it was a very old bottle carrier, the wood dividing each section was curved and quite attractive.

They took the wooden box home, and Jana's brother helped her to sand it until almost all the old paint was off. It looked smooth and antiqued. Then Jana scrubbed it clean, and her daddy put a nail in her bedroom wall. When the box was hung, with its bottom flat against the wall, it was a perfect display for her miniature collection with twenty-four separate cubicles.

Jana spent a whole afternoon arranging her most prized miniatures in the cubicles. Some she put by themselves, and others she put together if they belonged in the same category. For example, the ivory Buddha needed a cubicle all to itself; it seemed too important and aloof to share its space. The engineer and wooden train, however, went together cozily and companionably in the same compartment.

By nighttime, when Jana went to bed, she had her display box arranged to her complete satisfaction. It was directly across from her bed, so, as she drifted off to sleep, the last thing she saw was her miniature collection. In the dim illumination of her night light, she stared at a different cubicle each night, and she would have the most wonderful and curious dreams about what she saw, or thought she saw, before she went to sleep. They were almost like fairy tales that came true, because Jana believed in them. Her miniatures came to life and had extraordinary adventures, which I will tell to you.

THE SPANISH DANCER AND THE DISOBEDIENT SLIPPERS

Jana thought the Spanish Dancer was beautiful. She stood about two inches high, and was very fragile. She wore a red satin gown which had ruffles from the waist to the floor; each ruffle was trimmed in black lace. Her flashing eyes and sleek hair were also black. She carried an open fan which matched her gown of satin and lace.

Despite her finery, she always looked despondent, and Jana knew why. How can a dancer be happy when half of her foot is broken? The long gown hid the disfigurement, and Jana loved her all the more because of it. She only wished the Spanish Dancer could somehow accept herself as she was and not always seem to be longing for the impossible.

The dancer was on one side of Buddha; on his other side were the porcelain slippers from Germany. They both were gold and had pointed toes and slender little heels. Decorating the toe of one was a pink rose with each delicate petal opened out, whereas the other had a white butterfly perched atop the toe, its outspread wings etched in gold.

As Jana was in bed staring at the sad face of the Spanish Dancer, she thought she saw something move and heard a tapping sound from the slippers' compartment. As soon as she shifted her gaze to them, however, they were perfectly still! Looking once more at the dancer, the same thing happened, and again there was no movement when she quickly turned back to the slippers. This went on and on, her eyes moving back and forth between the dancer and the slippers, until they finally closed in deep sleep.

"Clickety, clack — what a beautiful night to dance," tapped the Butterfly Slipper.

"You tapping idiot! You almost started too soon. Think you could wait till everyone was asleep," scolded Rose Slipper, standing on its toe and turning slowly around. "The coast is clear. Let's leap out of here!"

And with that, they joyfully bounded out of their compartment, tip-toed past Buddha, and were just making ready to pirouette to the floor when they both happened to notice Spanish Dancer. A tiny tear was rolling down her cheek as she looked at them enviously.

The porcelain slippers stopped in mid-air, and clicked their heels together in thoughtful discussion.

Butterfly said, "It's a shame. Could we help?"

Rose said, "She's so lovely. I think we should."

Now, the German slippers never agreed upon anything, except upon their desire to argue. This time, however, they did reach a decision. They knew that the only way the weeping Spanish lady could ever again have the joy of dancing would be through their magic, so they waltzed into her cubicle and told her to please step into them.

"But you are much too big," she objected, "and how can I put my lame foot into a slipper? Oh, you are cruel to make sport of me this way." She began sobbing loudly, and the slippers became quite upset. They could hear the Engineer, who was directly under the Spanish Dancer, pleading with them to leave her alone, and they could feel the cold, disapproving stare of Buddha right through the wooden partition.

All the miniatures both feared and respected the ivory Buddha, except for the porcelain slippers when they were in a dancing mood. Then the low monotone of Buddha's voice rang through the night air, chilling the occupants of the display box. "Let her be."

"Let's go," said Butterfly Slipper, who really preferred a night of fun to thankless good deeds.

"No," persisted Rose Slipper, ignoring Buddha's warning. "Now, dear little dancer, just trust us, for we have magic powers. Sit down and stick out your feet. It doesn't matter what condition they're in. You'll see."

After a moment's thought, Spanish Dancer decided to oblige since the slipper spoke with such certainty. As soon as she extended her feet, the slippers put themselves on her, and their magic began. They shrank in size until they fit her perfectly, even molding comfortably to her broken foot! She stood up and took a few tentative steps, and when she realized that she wasn't limping, she threw her head back and laughed with joy.

Then the German slippers took her on a merry dance down to the floor, pausing at each level of the display box so that she could give an aerial performance for the others. The first

stop was in front of the Engineer's compartment, and here she danced her best. They had always sensed the presence of each other (she had felt his compassion and he had been aware of her unhappiness), but they had never seen each other till the slippers danced her in front of him.

Butterfly and Rose were very obedient at this point; they let the Spanish Dancer twirl and kick up her heels. They let her sing her passionate Spanish songs as she flirted with her sparkling black eyes while coyly hiding the rest of her face with her fluttering fan. She lifted her ruffled skirt and did high kicks; she did graceful movements with her arms outstretched, clicking her fingers in time to her singing. She was filled with the rapture of doing what she enjoyed the most.

The Spanish Dancer felt the admiring eyes of the Engineer, and was pleasantly surprised at finding him so strong-looking and handsome. He stood tall and proud next to his wooden train. She was oblivious to the anger of Buddha, who was unable to see her from his position and who didn't approve at all of the slippers' antics. She could have danced in front of the Engineer all night, but Butterfly and Rose were tiring of letting her lead them. They'd never done a Spanish dance before, and at first it had been fun to learn, but now they had other ideas.

So down they stepped to the next cubicle as the dancer waved a sad farewell to the Engineer with her fan, for she had no power to stop the impulsive slippers. They took a moment to kick the miniature mandolin into wakefulness and ordered it to play for them. It was made out of a tiny walnut shell half and had a carved wooden neck and tightly drawn hair-thin strings.

"Let her dance for me," pleaded the Swan from his cubicle next to the mandolin. He, too, was broken and felt a great sympathy for the lovely dancer. Above Swan was Rooster, who slept through everything until morning. The Spanish Dancer was eager to perform for all the occupants of the display box, but as soon as Butterfly and Rose heard the lilting melodies from Mandolin, they became completely independent of her. Down they leaped to the floor, and each did its own version of dancing to the music. The trouble was, as usual, they didn't agree.

"It's a waltz!" Butterfly would say, beginning an easy one-two-three step.

"Oh, good — a tango!" Rose would answer, doing a much faster step.

Then Butterfly would start a fox trot, while Rose sashayed into a square dance.

Poor Spanish Dancer! They went on and on with her through the night, till her legs felt they would break as her foot had long ago. When Rose Slipper began a polka, while Butterfly was still doing the jitterbug, she knew she had to make them stop. Her hair was no longer slickly pulled back; it was hanging loose and in disarray. She had dropped her fan many hours before, and she was damp with perspiration. All her grace and agility were gone. She felt like a helpless rag doll, being torn apart by the whim of these senseless, disobedient slippers.

"Stop! I order you!" she shouted, but to no avail as Butterfly began a toe ballet and Rose decided to rumba.

"Stop!" commanded Buddha with his hollow, ringing voice; but the slippers were too far away to hear or care.

"Stop! I beg of you!" Spanish Dancer pleaded, crying more than she had when the slippers had first taken pity upon her. "I never, never want to dance again! If you'll just take me back and get yourselves off my feet, I'll never again be sorry that I can't dance."

Butterfly and Rose stopped in their tracks. They shuffled along uncertainly, trying to tap a decision from each other.

The Miniature Display

"Do you suppose she means it?" asked Rose.

"I thought we were giving her the time of her life. I told you she'd be ungrateful," Butterfly grumbled, stubbing its toe.

"Well, maybe we'd better take her back. She looks awfully tired to me." Rose Slipper was very concerned when it saw how disheveled Spanish Dancer had become.

"If she'll never want to dance again — well, at least we won't have to listen to her crying anymore," said Butterfly Slipper, with one last high kick to emphasize that accomplishment.

"O.K. It's almost morning, anyway. I hear Rooster flapping his wings and getting ready to crow. Let's call it a night and get back to our own size. I feel scuffed and worn out myself," acknowledged Rose.

They slowly climbed, as if by an invisible stairway, until they came to the display box. As they passed Walnut Mandolin, they motioned for him to stop, which he happily did since he'd been strumming all night and they hadn't followed his music anyway. As they ascended past Engineer, he was left deeply concerned about the condition of his beloved Spanish Dancer.

They took her into her cubicle and sat her down, kicking themselves off her feet. As they grew to their normal size, they did a "Shuffle-off-to-Buffalo" step, in farewell, detouring around the furious Buddha, who felt very protective of Spanish Dancer, and finally settling to rest in their own compartment where they slowly tapped themselves to sleep.

Spanish Dancer, exhausted though she was, stood up and smoothed her hair and ruffles. "I will never want to dance again, ever!" she vowed, and she meant it.

Engineer smiled when he heard her, but Buddha frowned because the slippers had ignored him. Spanish Dancer wasn't angry with the disobedient German slippers, for she knew they had done her a great service.

The first thing Jana did when she awoke was to go to her display box and take out Spanish Dancer. She looked the same, except her dress felt a little damp and her face no longer seemed sad. In fact, she looked very content — but something was missing. Jana looked down and found it on the carpet, immediately (since she never had trouble discovering tiny things). She picked up the teeny, weeny fan which was the size of a capital letter "V", placed it back into the hand of the Spanish Dancer, and carefully put her back into her compartment.

THE SWAN ORNAMENT

The oldest miniature in Jana's display box was the swan. It was at least thirty-five years old. It had been her mother's favorite Christmas ornament from childhood on, and now it was Jana's. They used to always keep it carefully wrapped and packed in a box with all the other ornaments until last year, when Jana begged her mother to let her keep it with her miniatures, since it was so tiny. Although it was broken and dull, it was very precious to the family; and Jana took especially good care of it. She was happy when she was able to place it in her display box, for she knew it would be safe there.

One night in December, Jana was trying to go to sleep but couldn't. She was too excited counting the days until Christmas, and her heart and mind raced with holiday expectations. She tried to calm herself by remembering the story her mother, Lynn, had told her about the old swan and how it had broken the year Jana was born. She wondered what his life had been like all those years packed away in the ornament box awaiting each Christmas. She drifted to sleep thinking of how the days must have dragged for him until he could feel the holidays approaching ...

It was very dark inside the box of Christmas ornaments. The box had been stored in the

The Green Tiger's Caravan

attic a long time, and there was no way of telling how many days had gone by. Inside the box, day and night seemed the same, but the summer was warmer and the winter cooler.

It was quite chilly now, and the old ornament was bursting with excitement. "Any day now, my dear family will be taking us down to the living room and unwrapping us one by one."

He was the oldest ornament in the box. Most of the others were bright, shiny balls; but he was very different. He was in the shape of a swan. Long, long ago, when he was new, he was a sparkling pink with glossy white feathers for a tail. He'd had designs that looked like frosted sugar on his wings.

The old swan sighed when he thought of how he must look now, compared to the other pretty ornaments. He had become duller with each passing year; his sugar frosting had all but disappeared; and, worst of all, he had lost his tail last year! It had just fallen apart from old age.

"They won't want to keep me much longer," he thought. "Even the back of the tree will be too good for me."

He wiped away a tear and took some comfort in remembering that he always was wrapped more carefully than the other ornaments and that dear Lynn always placed him on the top of the pile before closing the box, as if she didn't want him crushed by the weight of the others.

Lynn had been just a baby when he was brand new. He loved to remember each Christmas and how she had grown with every year. This was how he passed the time during those long days of waiting, in the box, for the next Christmas.

When Lynn was two years old, she began to notice him, calling him "Boodie", for she couldn't say "birdie". When she was three, she couldn't wait for him to be unwrapped and wanted to put him on the tree herself. And each year after that, the swan had been her favorite ornament.

He thought back to the time when she had been seven years old, a freckled schoolgirl with pigtails. She used to secretly take him off the tree and play pretend games with him. Once he had been the pet swan of a beautiful princess. Another time he had been changed into a swan by a wicked ogre, but a kiss from a lovely maiden turned him back into a young prince. It had been so much fun, and she had always been very careful not to hurt him.

When she was nine, it had been an unhappy year. Lynn sat in a chair surrounded by pillows through most of the holidays. She was too sick to play with him and just looked at him sadly. Her face was so thin and pale, and she had a terrible cough. She was supposed to have her tonsils out as soon as Christmas was over, and he spent that whole next year worrying about her and praying that when the box was again opened, she'd be there, bright and cheerful.

And, sure enough, when the year finally had passed, and it was another Christmas; she was so healthy and lovely, he wished he could fly through the air with the joy he felt. That year Lynn had a slumber party around the tree. She had proudly pointed him out to her girlfriends, which made up for her not playing pretend games with him anymore.

She started changing so much the next few years, that he always had a happy surprise when he saw her. He would spend the year in the box wondering how much she had grown. She lost her freckles; she wore her hair loose and long; and always, each year, she became prettier, like a blossoming flower.

Then, when she was sixteen, she brought a boy named Michael home for a holiday dinner. They sat under the Christmas tree doing a jigsaw puzzle, and Lynn took the swan off the branch to show to Michael. He held the fragile swan so gently and seemed to understand

80

The Miniature Display

how much it meant to Lynn. The swan looked forward to seeing Michael again the next year and was happy to find he was there. In fact, Michael spent more and more time with Lynn each Christmas, and the swan saw the look of love in their eyes, and it warmed his heart.

Finally there was the special Christmas when Michael asked Lynn to be his wife. When she said, "Yes!" the swan knew that the glow of lights on the tree couldn't match the glow of happiness in their smiles.

During the following year, he could feel the box of ornaments being moved, but he knew it wasn't time for Christmas quite yet. He heard a strange voice saying, "Where do you want this, Lady?" and then he heard Lynn say, "Put it in the attic, but be VERY CAREFUL."

The next time he was taken out of the box, he saw that he was in a new house and that it belonged to Lynn and Michael. They lovingly put him on the tree together, and he was thrilled to still be a part of their lives.

And so the swan passed his days in the dark box, reliving the years through which he'd watched Lynn grow from a sweet baby to a playful schoolgirl, then a blossoming teen with sparkling eyes, and finally a happy wife. And with all the changes, he still felt she had a special place in her heart for him. She was sad when he lost his tail, but she still put him near the front of the tree and wrapped more tissue around him than ever when she put him away.

That had been just last year, but it had been a happy year, anyway. That Christmas, there had been a little puppy under the tree. His name was Waggles because he wagged his tail so much, and the swan loved him. He looked forward to seeing Waggles again this year and watching his tail go full speed with the excitement of Christmas.

And now the time was coming closer; he could feel it. He even thought he smelled the wonderful fragrance of a pine tree in the house. Then, finally, one day he felt the box being lifted and carried. He heard their happy voices, mingling with the beautiful Christmas music they played each year as they decorated the tree. He smelled the hot popcorn and cold cider they always had at this time. This was so worth waiting for! The most wonderful time of the year, and he was a part of it!

Patiently, he waited while Lynn and Michael set the tree in the stand and took the longest time to figure out which side looked the best. He laughed as he heard the usual sounds of Michael grunting and grumbling while arranging the lights, and then Lynn said, "Now let's have the fun of putting on the ornaments!" That meant they were ready for him!

The top of the box was being opened, and he could see the brightly colored Christmas lights through his tissue wrapping. Then he felt the soft hands he knew so well pick him up and gently unwrap him.

"Ah, here's our swan," said Lynn, smiling at him as if she were a little girl again. She looked more radiant than he'd ever remembered.

She placed him on one of the lower branches, but near the front of the tree as always. Just then, Waggles, who had been quivering with excitement, bounded forward.

"Look out — " Lynn began, but it was too late. The swan felt a part of his back cracking as he fell to the floor. It was the part that held the prong for the hook. In his eagerness, Waggles' tail had knocked the swan from the tree, pulling the prong from its fragile back; and now the few pieces that had held it in place lay like bits of broken eggshell near Waggles' paws. The poor dog licked the swan to let him know that he was ashamed of himself. His tail wasn't wagging now. It was between his legs, for he had loved the swan, too.

The old ornament felt sorry for Waggles and tried to let him know that being frisky and excited wasn't his fault. He knew, though, that this meant the end for him. Without a tail, without a sparkle, and now with no way of hanging, he knew that his Christmas would be spent in the trashcan.

Then Lynn, after petting Waggles in forgiveness, slowly picked up the swan and turned him around, looking at all sides of him with tenderness. "Well, he's still in one piece, but we can't hang him on the tree anymore," she said sadly. He felt the end had come, but he had enjoyed so many Christmases that he tried to be brave.

Suddenly, Lynn's eyes lit with an idea. "Wait," she said, "I think there's a way our swan can still be on the tree and in a more special place than ever."

The swan felt his heart jump and couldn't believe what he'd heard. They still wanted him! But how would they put him on the tree?

Lynn left the room for a while, and when she came back, she held what looked like a nest.

"I made this from some of the pine twigs we cut off our tree," she told Michael. "They say that if you have a bird in a nest on your Christmas tree, you'll have good luck all through the year."

She gently placed the swan in the nest and tucked it snugly in the branches at the top of the tree, where he could look down on his beloved family. He had the place of honor and knew it was his from then on! He looked up at the ceiling and gave a little prayer of thanks.

And as if his happiness were not complete enough, he had the most wonderful surprise of all! For when he looked down again, there was Lynn holding a baby wrapped in a pink blanket. She must have been born during those days he was in the attic box awaiting Christmas. Lynn held her up to him, saying, "Look at your pretty swan, my darling Jana!"

The swan thought of how wonderful it was going to be to watch another little girl grow up — one who would gently put him in the nest each year and, as she got taller, would place him at the top of the tree! He was so happy that a tear in his eye caught all the lights from the tree and made him shine with love.

Jana overslept because she'd been so deep in her dream about the swan. While she hurriedly dressed for school, she talked to the old ornament very tenderly.

"Don't worry, you'll always be my favorite ornament, too. And you'll get to see me grow every day, right here in this room, instead of just at Christmastime."

As she went out the door, she softly called back, "And then, some day, you'll see my children."

ILLUSTRATED PRIMAL ACROSTIC

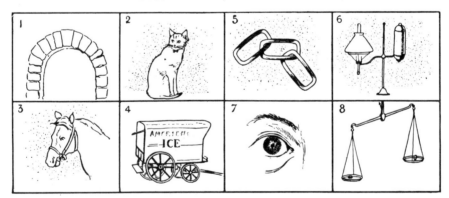

WHEN the eight objects in the above illustration have been rightly guessed, and the names placed one below another in the order given, the initial letters will spell the name of a Greek legendary warrior.

Answer, p. 88

A Christmas Story

by Caren Short
illustrated by Eric Hanson

The clip-clip-clop, clip-clop-clop, clop-clip-clop sound of the horses' hooves hitting upon the cobblestones had a very reassuring and warm effect upon Roger Dunne. It was good that *something* could affect him like that. After all, here it was, one of the most bone-tingling Christmas Eves he could remember, and what had he been doing? Certainly not sitting by the warm fire sipping eggnog and telling the children about Father Christmas as he enjoyed doing. Oh, no. Roger Dunne had been sent to Surrey to finish a business transaction. Indeed, he had been lucky to finish the business and get back in time for a Christmas celebration of any sort, but, dash it all! It was Christmas!

Roger banged his cane against the top of the cab.

"Driver. Driver!"

The barrier between the warm inside of the cab and the chilled outside of the world was removed. It was replaced by the red face of the driver.

"Sir?"

"Driver, is there a faster route to follow to reach home? I am getting most anxious."

The driver studied the gentleman's face for a moment.

"Sir, the only way to do that, sir, is to go right smack dab through the middle of London."

The driver eyed him passively, knowing that gentle folk do not go through that part of the city but anxiously hoping that this man would. After all, he, too, wanted to celebrate Christmas. Therefore, when Roger answered, "Well, then, get on with it," the driver gave him a hearty, "Yes, sir!" slammed the barrier in place, urged the horses on, and indulged in a rather boisterous rendition of "Joy to the World."

Roger smiled at the song. He gathered his greatcoat and scarf closer about him as a protection against any sudden contact with the cold air from outside. He leaned back and thought about the following day with his family and friends. There would be laughter, singing, a huge meal, gifts, and, of course, church services. The combination of the newly gained warmth, thoughts of tomorrow, and the clip-clop of the horses' hooves lulled Roger into a soft but delicious sleep.

He was awakened by the voices of London's street people. They were doing lots of heavy drinking, eating, singing, dancing, and laughing. It sounded like a fine time was had by all.

Roger wanted to look out the window and see if he recognized anyone. He had been born in this section of the city. Why, his mother and sister ... "God rest their souls," he sighed. They were both taken with the fever some fifteen years ago. His mother supported them by doing laundry for some of the gentle folk. Sometimes, Roger would go along to help. One of the families she worked for took a liking to Roger. They kept commenting on what a bright, good boy he was and how such a boy as he should be given a chance at a better life. After the deaths of his mother and sister, this family took Roger in. They clothed him, fed him, educated him; they all but adopted him. The gentleman even occasionally called him "son." His own father had run off shortly after the birth of Louise. His poor, gentle sister — she was much too frail to survive the hard life of the London backstreets. It was a hard life, but, by God, there were some fine times, too. Now he wanted very much to look for a familiar face.

A Christmas Story

Roger peeked out for an instant only but was greeted by taunts.

"Glory be! Hit's a gen'lmun!"

"Shall we courtsy to 'im?"

"Oo do y'suppose 'e's come callin' on?"

"For two shillin's 'e c'n come callin' on me!"

This was followed by raucous laughter. Roger dared not look out now. He smiled to himself. He remembered how it was when he was younger. The infrequent gentleman's carriage was always greeted by taunts such as these. If he dared to look out, he was invariably hit in the face by a flagon of beer, mud, or worse. "No, thank you," thought Roger. He could wait.

After a bit, Roger became aware of the pervading silence. There was something about the silence. He looked out, almost knowing what he would see. It was a very dark section of the area. It was where the people were housed. His eyes alighted on a tiny, boxlike house structure that seemed very familiar to him. It was quite dark, save for the faint flicker of light coming from the window. A quick memory flashed through him. Could it be? As the cab crossed the intersection, he noticed the names of the streets: Kingston and Blackberry. Yes, it was! Roger leaned back and let the memory wash completely over him.

It was a Christmas Eve much like this one. The weather was colder and more piercing than usual. Roger's mother had been asked by his future benefactor to act as a maid at a Christmas party for a little extra money. Roger and his sister were left on their own that Christmas Eve. Louise had gone to a friend's house for the evening, but poor Roger had nowhere to go. The little boy was quite lonely. He could think of nothing to do but wander about, peek in shop windows, and listen to the voices of happy people. This only made him more miserable.

Roger thought that this was the worst feeling that any boy could ever have. In hope of gaining some warmth, Roger huddled against the wall of a building and stuffed his hands as deep as he could into his pockets. He came upon the cheese and sausage his mother had given him. He fingered it, wondering when exactly would be a good time to eat it. A chorus of laughing voices broke in on Roger's thoughts, which was unfortunate for the little boy. The voices did nothing but remind Roger of his loneliness. Being only eight years old and being alone on this, of all nights, little Roger broke down and started crying.

A woman had been watching Roger from her window. Shaking her head sympathetically and clucking to herself, she disappeared from the window and emerged from the door, still in the act of throwing a heavy, tattered shawl about her shoulders. She crossed the street to where Roger was crying.

"'Ere now, deary. Wot's the matter with you?" her hoarse voice croaked.

Roger looked up and was visibly startled by what he saw. Here was one of the ugliest women he had ever seen. She looked almost like one of the witches he had heard about in fairy stories. He began to withdraw from the repulsive form, but there was something about her that struck him inside. Those eyes! Despite her overall ugliness, she had the friendliest pair of twinkling blue eyes Roger had ever seen. Encouraged by the friendly eyes, Roger told of his plight. The woman nodded in sympathetic understanding.

"I know 'ow you feel," she said, bobbing her head up and down. "I, like you, am all alone. 'Tisn't a very good feelin', eh?"

Roger shook his head in reply, at the same time trying to stifle a sob.

The eyes rested keenly on Roger while the jaws worked for a minute as if chewing on a piece of meat.

"Would you care to share yer Christmas Eve with me? ... I 'aven't much, but wotever I

85

have is yers."

Roger started to refuse, but something inside stopped him. The eyes pleaded softly with him.

"All right," he nodded shyly. "I'll go with you."

The two crossed the street to her home. It was quite small, but, as he was told, "It's big enough for one tiny lady."

Roger walked in the door and took in the entire room at one glance. There was a bed, a table, a chair, a stool, some utensils, some clothing, and a barely lit stove.

She noticed his glance and repeated what she said outside. "I 'aven't much, but wot I 'ave is yers."

Roger smiled his thanks. He was beginning to feel better. The warmth from the stove and the woman's friendly manner cheered him greatly.

A Christmas Story

The woman bustled about as though she were entertaining royalty. She moved a lighted candle to the table, poured ale for the two of them, and laid out some bread. His hostess didn't say anything, but Roger could tell that she was sorry that that was all she had. For lack of anything better to do, Roger put his hands in his pockets. His face exploded into a smile. He had forgotten about the cheese and sausage his mother had given him. He took the food out of his pocket and proudly laid it on the table.

"Well, well, well!" the woman clucked. "'Ere's a feast!" She gave Roger his cup of ale and raised her own for a toast. "'Ere's to a good Christmas for all, but mostly, deary, for you and me."

The woman and the boy stood smiling at each other, bathed in the warmth of Christmas.

The voice of the driver broke in on Roger's thoughts to announce that the destination had been reached. Roger smiled at the remembrance of his very special Christmas. He paid the driver and got out of the carriage, watching for a moment as the horses clip-clopped merrily down the street.

The door to the house had opened. Roger was not to be greeted by the children as he had hoped. Sarah, the housemaid, was at the door. She gave him a polite curtsey.

"Good evening, Sir. Merry Christmas. It's good to have you home."

"Thank you, Sarah. It's good to be home." He stood in the hall for a moment and waved off her attempt to take his hat and coat.

"The missus and the children didn't know when you would be home, so they accepted a dinner invitation from the Browns. You have been asked to join them if you're not too tired after your journey."

"All right, Sarah. That will be all."

Roger went into the main room and stood in front of the Christmas tree. It was a magnificent tree. As he looked at it, he kept thinking of the woman and the Christmas of long ago. Impulsively, Roger grabbed a bauble from the tree and went to the kitchen for some food and wine. He, then, went outside to hail a cab and order it to the corner of Kingston and Blackberry Streets.

He paid the driver, got out of the cab, and walked towards the small house. His heart was beating wildly with anticipation. After all, it had been twenty years. She may not be there any longer. He drew in his breath and knocked on the door.

A wizened, silver-haired old lady with friendly blue eyes answered the door. She was quite surprised to see a gentleman at the door and curtsied as best as her old bones would allow her.

Roger laughed with delight, pronounced her name like it was the only name in the world, and explained who he was. The old woman's eyes crinkled and moistened.

"Do come in," she said in her near extinct voice. "I 'aven't much, but wot I 'ave is yers."

Roger went in and looked about. He shivered. Absolutely nothing had changed. There was a bed, a table, a chair, a stool, some utensils, some clothing, and a barely lit stove. He bustled about while the old woman stood by and watched. She was too overcome to move. All she could do was clasp her hands and rock from side to side. Roger made the fire in the stove roar. He lit a candle and placed it on the table, along with the bauble from his Christmas tree. The food was arranged on the table and the wine was poured. Then Roger ceremoniously seated the woman in her chair. They raised their glasses.

"A toast," he said, gazing in the friendly eyes. "A toast wishing everyone a happy Christmas. But happiest of all, dear lady, is yours and mine."

Once again, the old woman and the young man smiled at each other, bathed in the warmth of Christmas.

ANSWERS

p. 9. RIDDLES
1. A needle and thread.
2. Because he has been to sea (see).
3. A hole.
4. Because they never saw it.
5. Because it has the most stories.
6. In the baseball park.
7. A river.
8. No(i)se.
9. Because it is apt to run down and strike one.
10. A promise.
11. (1) w-ink. (2) th-ink. (3) r-ink. (4) br-ink. (5) dr-ink. (6) m-ink.
12. When he pulls its ears.

p. 21. OMITTED LETTERS
Vacation. i, c, n, a, v, o, a, t

p. 29. BEHEADINGS
1. Clock-lock.
2. Page-age.
3. Shoe-hoe.
4. Chil-hill-ill.

p. 42. THE THREE RABBITS

p. 58. THE CARPENTER PUZZLED

An examination of this diagram will show how the square piece was cut from the board.

THE GRASPING LANDLORD

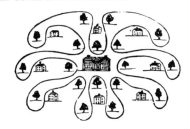

p. 60. WORD SQUARES

```
1. K I T E    2. S N O W    3. S A L T
   I R O N       N A M E       A J A R
   T O A D       O M E N       L A T E
   E N D S       W E N T       T R E E
```

p. 66. ANIMAL PUZZLE SUMS
1. C + goat − cat + P + hen + R − N = GOPHER.
2. Clock − lock + rat − R = CAT.

p. 82. ILLUSTRATED PRIMAL ACROSTIC
Achilles. 1. Arch. 2. Cat. 3. Horse. 4. Ice wagon. 5. Links. 6. Lamp. 7. Eye. 8. Scales.

The arrangement of the stories, art and entertainments in this book was the work of Helen Neumeyer.
The printing was done at
The Green Tiger Press.